MAYORAL GOVERNANCE IN DUBLIN

Challenges for Citizens, Politics and Policy

Withdrawn from Stock

Edited by
Deiric Ó Broin and Eoin O'Malley

GLASNEVIN
PUBLISHING

Published in 2019 by

Glasnevin Publishing
2nd Floor, 13 Upper Baggot Street
Dublin 4, Ireland
www.glasnevinpublishing.com

The cover image is a photograph of Dublin's coat-of-arms in City Hall on Dame Street taken by Joanna Travers from the Media Relations and Corporate Communications Office of Dublin City Council. This is the identifying emblem of the City of Dublin and has been in use in one form or another for at least 400 years. The full coat-of-arms shows three burning castles on a shield, flanked by two female figures.

One holds a scales depicting Justice (without the usual blindfold) - the other, a sword representing Law. Each holds an olive branch. Below the shield on a scroll is the motto of the city "Obedientia Civium Urbis Felicitas" which translates as "The Obedience of the citizens produces a happy city".

A Catalogue record for this book can be obtained from the British Library.

Papers used by Glasnevin Publishing are from well managed forests and other responsible sources.

ISBN: 978-1-908689-35-1

CONTENTS

LIST OF FIGURES

LIST OF TABLES

ACKNOWLEDGEMENTS

This book is the result of numerous discussions and collaborations with many people at various places over the course of the past two years and these have been immeasurably helpful. The editors would like to thank the members of the Board of Directors and Management Committee of NorDubCo, the School of Law and Government in Dublin City University, and the School of Transport Engineering, Environment and Planning in the Dublin Institute of Technology for their support, advice and intellectual stimulation.

The editors would also like to thank the students (past and present) of the BA Economics, Politics and Law, and MSc in Public Policy in the School of Law and Government in DCU, and BSc Spatial Planning, MSc Local Development and Innovation, MSc Sustainable Development and MSc Urban Regeneration and Development in the School of Transport Engineering, Environment and Planning in DIT, for their willingness to engage with so many of the ideas contained in the book.

Deiric owes a special debt of gratitude to the women in my life, my late mother who encouraged me to continue my education, Kathleen who put up with many late-night proofing and editing sessions and Sarah who, in her own unassuming way, persuaded me to complete the project so she could watch Elmo on the laptop. Deiric also acknowledges the many interesting, provocative, and at times, zealous discussions with his colleagues in the North Dublin Political Economy Discussion Group.

Finally, we would like to thank Katy Halpin for her design of the book's cover and Jordana Corrigan and Fidelma Joyce for their efforts in proofing the manuscript and our colleagues in Glasnevin Publishing for their patience and advice.

CONTRIBUTORS

Mark Callanan is a lecturer with the Institute c. . . . . .
His research interests include local government reform, participative
democracy, performance measurement and public sector reform, and
he is currently working on the question of economies of scale in local
government. Mark has published in a number of international journals
and is the co-editor of the standard textbook on Irish local government.
In 2010 he worked on secondment to the Department of Environment,
Community & Local Government to carry out work on behalf of the
Local Government Efficiency Review Group, which reported to the
Irish Government on potential cost savings and efficiencies within the
local government sector. Before joining the IPA, Mark worked with
Deloitte & Touche in Brussels. He is a graduate of University College
Dublin, the College of Europe in Bruges, and University College Cork.

Colin Copus is the Director of the Local Governance Research Unit in
the Department of Politics and Public Policy, De Montfort University
where he is a Professor of Local Politics. His academic interests are
central-local relationships and the constitutional status of local
government, localism, local party politics, local political leadership and
the changing role of the councillor. Colin has worked closely with
policy-makers and practitioners in central and local government. He
has published widely in academic journals. Colin's latest books are
entitled: *In Defence of Councillors*, published by Manchester University
Press; and, *Local Government in England: Centralisation, Autonomy and
Control*, Palgrave MacMillan. Colin was the editor of *Local Government
Studies* 2001 to 2013 and he has also served as a councillor on a London
Borough council, a county and a district council and three parish
councils.

Pauline Cullen is a lecturer in Sociology and Politics in the Department
of Sociology, Maynooth University. Her work examines civil society
mobilisation on social justice and gender equality at national and
European Union level, women's movements and gender and political
representation. Her work has been published in the Journal of Civil
Society, Social Movement Studies and Gender Work and Organization.
Her current research projects include gender knowledge production in
education, media and cultural industries, research on women's

representation in local governance and local development, ethnic minority women's activism on employment rights and the feminist mobilisation at EU level in the context of austerity and populism.

Lisa Marie Griffith is a historian of Dublin and early-modern Ireland and holds a PhD from Trinity College Dublin. She has published several essays on eighteenth-century Ireland and is author of *Stones of Dublin: A History of Dublin in Ten Buildings*. Along with Ruth McManus she edited *Leaders of the City: Dublin's First Citizens 1500-1950* (Four Courts Press, 2013). Her current research area is death and dying in Ireland, which encompasses a broad range of topics including the history of undertakers in Ireland. Along with Ciarán Wallace she is co-editor of *Grave Matters: Death and Dying in Dublin 1500 to the present* (Four Courts, 2016).

Colin Knox is Emeritus Professor of Comparative Public Policy at Ulster University and Professor of Public Policy in Nazarbayev University, Kazakhstan. His research interests include: public sector reform (local and international); local government; and, the evaluation of public policy. He is the author of *Devolution and the Governance of Northern Ireland* (Manchester University Press); co-author (with Professor Vani Borooah) of *The Economics of Schooling in a Divided Society: The Case for Shared Education* (Palgrave Macmillan); co-author (with Padraic Quirk) of *Public Policy, Philanthropy and Peace Building* (Palgrave Macmillan). He has worked on public sector reform in many developing countries including: Kazakhstan, Bangladesh, China, Georgia, Russia, and Latvia. Knox is a Fellow of the Academy of Social Sciences (FAcSS) and Fellow of the Higher Teaching Academy (FHEA).

Dermot Lacey has been a councillor since 1993 and served as Lord Mayor of Dublin in 2002-2003. He is Leader of the Labour Group on the Council. He is a former Chairperson of the Housing, Social and Community Affairs Strategic Policy Committee (SPC), the Arts and Youth SPC and the Protocol Committee. Uniquely he has served as Chairperson of the Dublin Regional Authority, the Southern and Eastern Regional Assembly and the Eastern and Midlands Regional Assembly. He is a member of the board of the Royal Hospital Voluntary Housing Association, the Dublin Town - Business

Improvement District Scheme and of several local community development boards. He was a founder member of the Beech Hill Housing Initiative. He is a former member of the Dublin City Vocational Education Committee/Education and Training Board and the Board of FÁS and the Dublin Docklands Development Council. He proposed the introduction of the 20% Social and Affordable Housing requirement in the Docklands area, a move that was followed by legislation across the State for all developments. He is a lifelong member of the Scout Movement.

Ruth McManus is a senior lecturer at the School of History and Geography, Dublin City University. She is the author of *Dublin 1910-1940, Shaping the City and Suburbs* (Four Courts Press, 2002) and *Crampton Built* (Four Courts Press, 2008), and co-editor with Lisa-Marie Griffith of *Leaders of the City, Dublin's First Citizens 1500-1950* (Four Courts Press, 2013).

Deiric Ó Broin is Director of NorDubCo, based in Dublin City University, and Senior Research Fellow in the School of Law and Government in DCU where he lectures in Irish politics. In addition, he lectures in local economic development and innovation at the School of Transport Engineering, Environment and Planning in the Dublin Institute of Technology. He is a graduate of the Dublin Institute of Technology (BA [Hons] and LLB), UCC where he obtained a MBS (Social Enterprise), Keele University, where he completed a MA (Research Ethics) and UCD, where he completed a MA (Politics and Economics) and a PhD (Political Theory). He is a Fellow of the Institute of Economic Development and Co-Convenor of the Local Government Specialist Group of the Political Studies Association of Ireland.

Orla O'Donnell is a Senior Research Officer at the Research Division of the Institute of Public Administration (IPA). Her primary work since joining the IPA in 1999 has been for the IPA Research Series and the Committee for Public Management Research. This has included studies of innovation, e-government, ethics, organisational development, organisational culture, decentralisation, flexible working arrangements, service level agreements and key performance indicators. In addition, she is a course director of the Diploma and Certificate in Civil Service and State Agency Studies and editor of the Local Authority Times. She is a graduate of UCD, BA (Hons) History and Economics, MA Economics, and MBS Management and Organisation Studies. Prior to joining the IPA, she was an Economic Research Officer for the Sligo County Council Economic Development Unit as part of the Sligo County Council-Omagh District Council Partnership Body and lectured Economics in the School of Business and Humanities at Sligo Institute of Technology.

Eoin O'Malley is the Director of the MSc in Public Policy at Dublin City University, where he is Associate Professor (senior lecturer in old money) in political science. His work is mainly on Irish politics, particularly cabinet government, and leadership in Ireland. He is currently working on a project on policy failure and policy success in Ireland.

Aodh Quinlivan is a lecturer in politics at the Department of Government in University College Cork, where he specialises in local government and public sector management. He is also the Director of UCC's Centre for Local and Regional Governance (CLRG) in UCC, which was established in 2016. He has written numerous articles, primarily on local government, which have been published in national and international academic journals. He is the author of six books, the latest of which was published in September 2017 – *Dissolved: The remarkable story of how Cork lost its Corporation in 1924.*

Oisín Quinn has been a practicing barrister since 1992. He became a Senior Counsel in 2008 and he specialises in employment and defamation law. For 10 years he also served in local politics on behalf of the Labour Party. He was elected to Dublin City Council in 2004 and following his re-election in 2009 he was elected as the 344th Lord Mayor of Dublin in June 2013. During his term as Lord Mayor he chaired the Forum on the establishment of an Office for a directly elected Mayor of Dublin.

PREFACE

Prof. Brian MacCraith

Dublin City is undergoing a significant transformation. By 2040 it is likely to be a city of almost 2 million people. Not only will it be the biggest city in Ireland, but it also aspires to become a Global City. A Global City must be more than a big city. It must be one that is open to all, welcoming and outward looking. It must aspire to being world-class in its design and services. It must not only be an economic powerhouse, but it should also be one that leads in terms of culture and creativity. A Global City requires governance structures that support continuous transformation and enable long-term decision-making as well as being able to face policy challenges. The challenges, many of which we already see, relate to how to make Dublin a Liveable City. Liveable cities create and foster communities where citizens can afford to live, where they do not expend too much time commuting, where they can enjoy a clean environment and vibrant public spaces to rest and spend time with family and friends. The Liveable City will be one with a resilient economy that provides ample opportunities for its citizens.

These are not ivory tower ideas, or challenges that we can postpone into a distant future. But attempts to deal with them can bring immediate conflicts. The welcome introduction of MetroLink in Dublin brings a solution to some of our mobility issues, but we can see already the significant disruption it can pose to community stakeholders. Delivering the Liveable City that Dublin aspires to be requires careful forethought and planning – an attribute for which we are not renowned – and a recognition that in most cases there may be no perfect solutions. But the perfect should not be the enemy of the good.

The question that this book debates is whether or not an executive Mayor can provide the governance structures that will enable Dublin to face these challenges. It looks at the earlier attempt to introduce an elected mayor, and examines the experiences of elected mayors elsewhere and asks if such models might work for Dublin. I will let the readers make up their own minds regarding the answers to these important questions!

As a key stakeholder in the development of Dublin, Dublin City University is proud to make a contribution to the debate on how

Dublin should be governed. We are particularly pleased that a number of our academic staff members from different Schools have contributed to the debate on the governance of Dublin. We are also pleased to play a role in the development of that part of Dublin in which DCU is based, as well as the broader Eastern Corridor region. At DCU we aspire to much more than Ivory Tower teaching. We aim to transform the lives of our students, by giving them access to world class teaching, from researchers whose reputation is known globally. Through the incorporation of St. Patrick's College, Mater Dei Institute and Church of Ireland College of Education into DCU, the acquisition of the All Hallows Campus, and the development of the DCU Alpha Innovation Campus, we have helped to make the Drumcondra-Glasnevin region into a hub of education, culture, science and technology. We are actively fostering a sustainable community that is known for its creativity.

Dublin can become both a Global City and a Liveable City, but this will not happen by accident. The City Fathers (and Mothers!) can make it happen. This volume can help us get there.

Brian MacCraith is President of Dublin City University.

FOREWORD

Cllr. Dermot Lacey

In a country that, according to many commentators, but mind you, not by many practitioners, is bedevilled by 'localism' and 'clientelism', a study and informed commentary of local government is remarkably rare.

It is noteworthy that while the national broadcasting service has correspondents on many other areas of Irish life it has none with a specific responsibility for local government. Indeed, there is a far higher likelihood of the public relations representative of an insurance company being interviewed by RTÉ on Dublin traffic than the Chairperson of the City Council's Traffic Committee.

Yet the truth is reform of our local government system could be the catalyst to transform Ireland. There are many different ways in which that can be achieved. What is needed, however, is imagination, political will and a willingness to stand up to the permanent government in the senior ranks of the civil service.

Sadly, with brief exceptions and interventions by Brendan Howlin TD, Noel Dempsey TD and John Gormley TD, and indications of same from Alan Kelly TD, successive Ministers for Local Government have simply done the bidding of the real masters in the Custom House. Former "reformers" seem to have lost that zeal when ministerial office beckoned. Nowhere was that fact demonstrated more than the travesty that was the shameful and dishonestly titled Local Government Reform Act, 2014.

To paraphrase Aodh Quinlivan, our approach to real reform has been a case of: "We will, we won't, we didn't, we might. We won't".

That is one of many reasons I welcome this publication. It seeks to bridge the gap between 'town and gown'. The public want reform. Poll after poll, survey after survey has shown that. They want it because they know the present system does not work. But the form of reform or the urgency of the reforms needed has not yet penetrated civic or media discourse and an academic publication such as this can only help.

The case set out herein demonstrates clearly that whatever about the rest of Ireland, Dublin, as Ireland's capital city, needs a longer-term mayor within a functioning local government system. Whether such a mayor is directly elected or not is arguable. A longer mandated term is the key. In this context when I refer to Dublin I mean the full county.

Dublin needs a political voice. Perhaps more than anything else Dublin needs someone who understands how things work or more accurately do not work and who will stand up for the city and county. While I accept that, in a phrase attributed to me, the task will be more than "facing down the Custom House", however, that will be a key element, in terms of establishing such a post and then in exercising it. Dublin needs someone who can be a political advocate and armed with the mandate of direct election is my preference. However, there could be other methods for selection. This book explores some of the options. In short, the Toronto model which provides for direct election as outlined below is my preference.

Many believe that we need more than the simple introduction of a directly elected mayor – they are right. A new mayor can and must drive further reform and the future of Dublin. The essential element is that the mayor would have the power and resources to do the job, and the commitment to do it effectively.

The contribution by Oisín Quinn on his experience as Chairperson of the Forum on the Establishment of the Office of Directly Elected Mayor of Dublin established under the 2014 Act is worth reading again and again for the range of possibilities explored and the political manoeuvring to ensure that the post would not be established. While, as a member, I accept the Forum proposals were perhaps too broad ranging, the manner in which the then Minister and Government determined that a vote of 98 votes in favour with 19 votes against was insufficient to make progress, was quite simply farcical and sickening.

Subsequent chapters outlining the challenges, obstacles, arguments for and against reforming our system are all illustrative of the huge mountains that will have to be climbed if we are to make progress. A clinging on to power, often incompetently used by central government is perhaps the greatest obstacle of all. Sadly we should not, and I do not, underestimate the political opposition of many TDs to reform because sadly, in many ways, reform of our local government system would benefit most of those TDs who want to be national politicians.

It must be clear to any interested citizen that our system of local government requires renewal and reform. Clear too must be the fact that local councils are directed, unofficially but in reality, by the chief executives not councillors, answerable to the Department and the permanent officials therein. That is the key to understanding our present problems and it must end if there is to be meaningful reform.

Three of the arguments outlined here, and elsewhere, against directly elected mayors are cost, 'celebrity' candidates, and a potential loss of power and a more constrained role for other elected councillors. In my view the first two are bogus and the latter can be dealt with through a rebalancing of powers. Properly structured, a longer term elected mayor, working with an enhanced Dublin regional authority, would see the need for many of the existing agencies reduced and/or incorporated into the mayoral structure, with significant savings and enhanced roles for the other elected members.

Further, on the 'celebrity' candidate issue, the answer is simple – we live in a democracy – let the people decide. I have great faith that the electorate will decide intelligently. Recent European and presidential elections have shown a reduction of the impact of 'celebrity' over the course of lengthy campaigns.

The absence of an independent source of funding was a major flaw in previous proposals and has not been addressed by the 'con job' that is the Local Property Tax. I have repeatedly called for the convening of a Forum on the Financing of Local Government and do so here again. The Forum comprising representatives of the political parties, the Association of Irish Local Government, the Local Authority Members Association and the social partners would be charged with recommending an overall system of financing with additional options available to councils should they choose to avail of them.

Appropriate financing is central to a strong, democratic and effective system of local government. It must form an integral part of any serious reform process.

While details of many of the proposed reforms are extensive, the essentials are not. They must include:

- An independent source of funding – not subject to the whims of the Department of the Housing, Planning and Local Government;
- Overhaul of the Local Government Act, 2014;
- Real controls and limitations on spending at local elections and an ethical framework that is robust;
- Re-establishing the Dublin Regional Authority as a directly elected assembly with approximately 24 members. The responsibilities of the Authority, working with the Mayor, should include:

- o Land use planning and strategic development;
- o Traffic and transport – it would be the Dublin Transport Authority;
- o Social and affordable housing;
- o The enhancement and protection of Dublin Bay, waterways and mountains;
- o Economic development and enterprise.
- The Authority would also have a co-ordinating and/or monitoring role in relation to county-wide services provided by agencies such as the Health Services Executive, the Education and Training Boards, Enterprise Ireland, the Garda Síochána and relations with other relevant bodies.

As I said at the outset Ireland can be transformed by a reformed local government system. It is long past time for better local government and long past time to 'Stand up for Dublin'. This publication makes a real contribution to that cause.

Cllr. Dermot Lacey
Cathaoirleach (2017-2018)
Eastern and Midland Regional Assembly

CHAPTER 1
INTRODUCTION

Deiric Ó Broin and Eoin O'Malley

Introduction

This book can be seen as a sister volume to *Local Dublin, Global Dublin: Public Policy in an Evolving City Region* (2010) and *Local Governance, Development and Innovation: Rebuilding Local Economies in Ireland* (2017). Both critically assessed the nature of the relationship between the economy of the Dublin city region and the key policy-making processes and institutions of governance in the region. A feature of this book, and those that preceded it, is our desire to combine academic insight with the knowledge and experience of those involved in public policy formulation at a variety of levels, and from different practitioner perspectives. As Hambleton notes this can be a "hazardous enterprise as scholars and practitioners tend to inhabit separate worlds" (2014: xiii). As a result, they can often, while speaking the same language, talk past each other to the disadvantage of both parties. We hope that this book helps consolidate and further the dialogue we have worked to nurture.

This introductory chapter details the broad civic and political context and focus of the book, broadly reviews the chapter themes, provides some background on the origins of the book and finally, suggests the possible contribution the book can make.

Setting the Civic and Political Context

Rousseau claims "houses make a town, but citizens make a city"[1] (1762: 68). Arguably cities have been to the forefront of democratic experimentation for millennia (Keane, 2009), indeed cities were the cradle of what became states and it was cities that made democracy necessary and possible. Today new challenges present themselves, challenges that have the potential to create "remarkable, new opportunities for bold and imaginative civic leaders" (Hambleton, 2014: 5). However, in a dynamic, fast moving environment these same

---

[1] The original text is: la plupart prennent une ville pour une cité, et un bourgeois pour un citoyen. Ils ne savent pas que les maisons font la ville, mais que les citoyens font la cité.

1

challenges may magnify the risk of failure and require cities to be well led. For many of the most critical services affecting humans happiness are to some extent controlled at the level of local authorities. The quality of housing, urban design, transport, the connectivity of communities are all affected by local policies. Local government is the level at which many of the collective action problems citizens face daily can be solved.

Some will argue that every generation believes it is facing near insurmountable challenges and living through tumultuous changes. Cities have always faced challenges. What is so different about now? The editors take the view that there are two distinct reasons why the current dynamic of change presents unprecedented challenges for those concerned with the governance of cities, globalisation and urbanisation.

As Gross and Hambleton note the "economic, political, social, environmental and cultural changes implied by the term 'globalisation' are truly startling" (2007: 1). These changes can at times appear overwhelming but civic leadership can provide the necessary competitive advantage to thrive in this fluid global system. The evidence suggests that urbanisation will create just as many challenges. Alongside globalisation it is and will remain a key driver of societal change, even more so in a political system and culture that remains so oriented to rurality, we must acknowledge that we live in a time where city leaders face unprecedented challenges. How Dublin's leaders and communities respond to these challenges, and the instruments they use, including redesigned public institutions like the mayoralty, is of enormous importance for the wellbeing of Ireland.

A recent Irish Times editorial notes:

> Cities are now unquestionably the engines of most countries' economies and need good governance if they are to attract inward investment and tourism. That's one of the main reasons for having directly elected mayors with real power to cut through layers of bureaucracy and get things done. Whatever about the respective talents of those who have held the office of mayor of London over the past 17 years, there is general agreement that it has been a success, not least in providing a recognised

spokesman for the city, with a range of powers to address its needs (15th December 2017).

The contributors to this volume share the editorial's premise but bring their own particular expertise and insights to suggesting solutions.

Background

This book draws together contributions from academics and practitioners in the public policy, Irish politics, local government and local development sectors who contributed to the Martin McEvoy Annual Conference *New Politics and Policy in the City – Mayoral Governance of the Dublin City Region* on Wednesday 14th September 2016 in Purcell House in the All Hallows Campus of Dublin City University. The conference examined potential models of mayoral governance and the implications of each for the region and its stakeholders.

The conference's keynote address was delivered by Professor Colin Copus, Professor of Local Politics at De Montfort University, and included contributions from Professor Colin Knox (Ulster University), Dr. Eoin O'Malley (Dublin City University), Orla O'Donnell (Institute of Public Administration), Dr. Aodh Quinlivan (University College Cork), Dr. Pauline Cullen (Maynooth University) and Dr. Mark Callanan (Institute of Public Administration).

In addition to the formal academic and public policy contributions the conference was devised to include a very significant input from councillors, including a number of former mayors and lord mayors. This took two distinct forms, the first was a Practitioner Roundtable facilitated by former Dublin City Councillor and Alderman Pat Carey[2]

---

[2] Carey first entered local politics in 1985 when he was elected to Dublin City Council for the Finglas area. He remained on the council until the abolition of the dual mandate in 2003. He was elected as a Fianna Fáil TD for the constituency of Dublin North-West at the 1997 general election, was re-elected at the 2002 general election and the 2007 general election, when he was appointed as Minister of State at the Department of Community, Rural and Gaeltacht Affairs with special responsibility for Drugs Strategy and Community Affairs. In 2008, he was appointed as Minister of State at the Department of the Taoiseach (Government Chief Whip) by Brian Cowen TD. He was also appointed Minister of State with special responsibility for Active Citizenship. On 23rd March 2010, he was appointed as Minister for Community, Equality and Gaeltacht Affairs. On 20th January 2011, Carey was also appointed

and included representatives of Sinn Féin (Cllr. Mícheál Mac Donncha), Fianna Fáil (Cllr. Paul McAuliffe), Fine Gael (Cllr. Norma Sammon), Labour (Cllr. Dermot Lacey), Greens (Cllr. Roderic O'Gorman), Social Democrats (Cllr. Gary Gannon), Workers Party (Cllr. Éilis Ryan), Independents (Cllr. David O'Connor) and the People Before Profit Alliance (Cllr. John Lyons). It was intended that every political party represented on one of the four Dublin local authorities would be present but unfortunately representatives of the United Left Alliance and the Anti-Austerity Alliance were not able to attend on the day. The second councillor input came from a structured plenary session, again facilitated by Pat Carey. The conference was also recorded and made publicly available which in turn allowed contributors to revisit points made by each other and incorporate them into the chapters in this edited volume.

A number of sometimes distinct, sometimes overlapping, and sometimes conflicting themes emerged from the conference and the subsequent discussions. The first theme relates to the importance of leadership, quite simply, "local leadership matters" (Hambleton, 2014: 5). It can make the critical difference to the quality of life in Dublin. A key argument of many contributors, though not all, is that what makes the directly elected mayoralty so attractive as a public institution is that it facilitates better city leadership by making city leaders and their work more transparent and by attracting different types of civic leader to the role than the situation to date.

The second theme reflects Ireland's seeming lack of regard for the local tier of governance. Taken in conjunction with the strong centralising dynamic within the Irish state, a number of contributors highlight the potential and likely obstacles to implementing models of mayoral governance, in particular the politico-cultural and institutional reform constraints.

The third theme reflects a significant cleavage among the contributors and relates to the prioritisation of directly elected mayors as a reform. While no contributor actively argued against the introduction of a directly elected mayor, and nearly all saw it as a welcome institutional reform, many contributors argue there are a

---

as Minister for Transport, following the resignation of Noel Dempsey TD. On 23rd January 2011, he was also appointed as Minister for Communications, Energy and Natural Resources, following the resignation of Eamon Ryan TD.

number of very significant reforms necessary to adequately equip local government in Ireland to meet the challenges it faces. A directly elected mayor, while welcome, is secondary to the items on the empowerment agenda.

The final theme emerging from the conference and the related dialogue does not reflect a consensus but is distinct and robust in its articulation, simply put Ireland should grasp the nettle and introduce directly elected mayors. As Colin Copus and Aodh Quinlan so succinctly put: just do it. There is an argument to be made that the current system of city/county chief executives was introduced in this manner, first Cork (1929), Dublin (1930) and then the rest of the country (1940). Is it time for such an approach again?

Origins

The book has its genesis in the annual Martin McEvoy Conference run by NorDubCo in Dublin City University (DCU). The conferences were organised and led by Deiric Ó Broin (NorDubCo) and Eoin O'Malley (DCU) in late 2016 and reflect a key aspect of NorDubCo's mission in the region, and the key role played by the university as a generator of knowledge.

NorDubCo is a coalition of public stakeholders established in 1996 to advance social, economic and civic innovation in the North Dublin region. Its members currently include Dublin City University, Dublin City Council, Fingal County Council, Dublin Northwest Area Partnership and Blanchardstown Area Partnership. The shared belief underpinning NorDubCo's establishment was that local government, local development agencies, the local university, local civil society organisations and local communities working together could make a difference to the region. At that time a very specific set of challenges faced the region and NorDubCo was configured to address those challenges. The period of prolonged economic growth and subsequent crises has changed many of the issues facing the region. In some cases, old issues are at least partially resolved or no longer as problematic. In others, changes in the economy have created a completely new set of issues to be addressed by the members of NorDubCo.

Throughout this period, NorDubCo has worked to advance social, economic and civic innovation in the region. As part of this it has worked to create a positive vision for community and working life for the region, a vision that seeks to embrace all of the region's communities. In operationalising this vision, NorDubCo's work has a number of distinct objectives. Of particular relevance is its contention, reflecting that of our stakeholders, that the region needs to develop a more inclusive policy debate and promote new thinking to influence the social, economic and civic environment.

In working towards these objectives NorDubCo works with representatives from a wide variety of civil society organisations, the business community, local government, the local development sector, public representatives (both local and national), education establishments (secondary, further and higher), the media, and state and semi-state institutions. The development of these relationships allows NorDubCo to facilitate a broad range of policy discussions among various stakeholders.

Underpinning these efforts is the belief that a fundamental challenge facing North Dublin is to overcome barriers to shared decision–making. This requires a climate conducive to negotiated governance, that is the involvement of variable networks of communities, civil society actors and other stakeholders in the relevant policy formulation and decision-making processes. Developing this form of governance involves addressing the issues of building and sustaining a social and civic environment facilitative and supportive of such a process. Such inclusive decision-making must also be responsive to both the long-term and immediate needs of communities, as well as the infrastructural and developmental requirements of enterprise in the region. It requires paying particular attention to inclusion and participation of the most disadvantaged.

As a contribution to the development of such a form of negotiated governance NorDubCo devised a Public Dialogue Programme in conjunction with our colleagues in the School of Law and Government in Dublin City University. This programme of activities is based on an understanding that civic engagement is the foundation of a thriving, vibrant civil society and a recognition that a space for dialogue about issues of public importance is often lacking. It is our earnest hope that NorDubCo's Public Dialogue Programme contributes to the addressing of these issues.

An important component of our programme is the annual Martin McEvoy Conference. The conference commemorates the former chairperson of NorDubCo. Martin served as Chairperson of NorDubCo from 1999 until 2007 and his commitment was both unceasing and constructive. He always played a pivotal role in our work. Whether it was sailing, his beloved Suttonians, business or local development, he was professional, dedicated and committed. He served with the Tolka Area Partnership as chairperson for their first five years and in the process supported hundreds of local people in setting up businesses or finding worthwhile employment. Martin was a founding member and former President of the North Dublin Chamber of Commerce and in addition he was an active member of the Council of the Dublin Chamber of Commerce. He also chaired the Fingal Enterprise Board, again supporting scores of new businesses to get started and grow. He served as chairperson of two boards of community initiatives in Corduff and Ladyswell in West Dublin. One provided a support service to elderly residents in the area and the other oversaw the establishment of a local youth and sports facility. All of this was after he had officially retired. Martin represented everything that was positive about the business community in North Dublin. He believed it was his community of which he was an integral part and he should serve as best he could in helping it develop. In a very practical way he believed in the common good and worked for it in a variety of ways, often with thanks and recognition, often without.

As an organisation we were diminished by Martin's untimely death. We lost a great friend and colleague with his passing. He had time for everyone and treated everyone equally. He will be remembered fondly for the genuine person that he was and it was a privilege for those of us fortunate enough to work with him. As a way of commemorating Martin, NorDubCo's board of directors decided to rename our annual conference in his memory.

We feel it was appropriate because, in addition to his practical commitment to help build the capacity of communities, Martin McEvoy was intensely curious about ideas and thought the conference, and its audience of politicians, students, public servants and community activists engaged in debate and, more often than not, disagreement, was a great addition to the region. As he often observed, over a coffee after a particularly intense debate, 'this type of discussion changes the way people see problems'.

We aim to continue in this vein for many years to come. The conference has been running since 2001 and each conference addresses issues of contemporary concern. As noted earlier, the aim is not just to present information but to develop a dialogue between presenter and audience and amongst the audience itself, in order to develop a fuller, more robust and shared understanding of the various issues under discussion. It was in this context that Deiric Ó Broin and Eoin O'Malley devised the parameters for the chapters in this volume. Three chapters were not part of the conference but we included them as we feel they add particular value. Quinn's provides a rich and contemporary set of practitioner insights and experience from the coalface of recent efforts to introduce a directly elected mayor in Dublin and McManus and Griffith's provides a very useful historical contextual framework for analysing the potential consequences for existing ways of doing business of the introduction of a directly elected mayor. Ó Broin's chapter details the background to much of the opposition to directly elected mayors and the likelihood of overcoming the obstacles to its introduction. We are also conscious that there are a number of areas the contributors and the related discussions didn't cover, for example the impact of a directly elected mayor on existing political parties, or whether the model could contribute to efforts to build urban resilience (Coaffee and Lee, 2016) and address the impacts of climate change, or the potential to attract groups that currently don't engage, i.e. young people or socio-economically marginalised communities. Unfortunately, these are the constraints that arise in an initiative of this type, you only notice what you didn't discuss after the event.

We hope that the arguments advanced in this book will provide ideas and insights that can support the development of new thinking about how to advance the appropriate governance arrangements for the Dublin region. As noted above the book aims to engage academic work in real policy decisions and to link the work of the university to the world of practice. In this context the book's aim is not to provide solutions but to help the reader revise and assess their own ideas.

CHAPTER 2
DUBLIN'S LORD MAYOR: A HISTORY

Ruth MacManus and Lisa-Marie Griffith

Introduction

The office of mayor was created by a charter granted to the city of Dublin in 1229 and from its foundation it has been shaped by national, colonial, religious and economic forces. It has also been a marker of civic change. How the office was run, who held the office and under what conditions can tell us much about the history of the city and country at large. This chapter charts some of the most important changes to have occurred within the office of Lord Mayor, including significant pieces of legislation that improved or restricted it, as well as examining the duties undertaken by the Lord Mayor. Under the charter of 1229, the freemen of the city of Dublin were given the right to elect a mayor each year to preside over the city through a corporation (Griffith and MacManus, 2013: 9). This made the mayor of Dublin the city's first citizen. Charters were one of the methods used by the English monarchy to gain the favour of Irish cities from the medieval period to the seventeenth century and they were important not just for the office but for the city at large. Under an Elizabethan charter of 1548, Dublin was established as a County Borough and this increased the powers of Dublin Corporation within the city boundaries (Lennon, 1989: 207). During the restoration, when war-torn Dublin was returning to normality, the office was elevated to that of Lord Mayor, a position first held by Daniel Bellingham in 1665. While this was achieved through a charter from Charles II, it had much to do with the influence of the Duke of Ormond, who had spent considerable time in Europe and was keen to see Dublin expand and develop into a first-rate European city.[3]

The corporation evolved alongside the city guilds. Indeed, these two bodies were quite intertwined with the guilds holding direct representation within Dublin Corporation so as to represent the interests of their trade. In fact, all corporation members were guild men. One of the landmark changes in the corporation occurred in 1840 when the Guilds were dissolved (Clark, 2013: 108). This act of

---

[3] Ormond was also responsible for laying out the Phoenix Park and introducing many other of the city's innovations from this period (Redmond, 2013: 63-73).

dissolution was in fact intended to reform the corporation. In the aftermath of Catholic emancipation, the guilds had refused to open their membership up to Catholics and the only way to facilitate the entrance of Catholics to the corporation was through this measure. This led to one of the most radical changes in corporation membership as families with a historic hold on offices lost seats to new Catholic entrants. Religion was a powerful force affecting the corporation; the other noteworthy feature of the office was gender. The office has been held overwhelmingly by men. The first woman to be elected to office was Kathleen Clarke in 1939 (Litton, 2013: 166). In total, just eight women have held the office of Lord Mayor in its history showing a disappointing lack of gender equality which is reflected in wider Irish politics (Dublin City Council, 2017). The Local Government Act, 2001 which legislated for a directly elected mayor of Dublin to come into effect in 2004, promised to become another landmark moment in the history of the office, but it failed to materialise. However, the proposal to introduce a directly elected mayor is still under active consideration and is discussed in the final sections of the chapter.

Role of the Mayor

The primary duty of Dublin's mayor was as chair of Dublin's Corporation. The corporation's duties which evolved from the thirteenth century included providing lighting, regulating market places, measurement of weights, applying tolls and taxes, building and maintaining city walls and roads and collecting rubbish. Most of these jobs did not fall directly on the corporation but were managed by sub-contractors who, for a fee paid by the corporation, undertook this work themselves. The city's income was generated by taxes on goods sold within the city's markets and, during the medieval period, by tolls into the city. With so much of the corporation's work focused on financial management, it is not surprising that this body was made up of members drawn from the city's trade and financial community or, more specifically, Dublin's guilds. There were twenty-four guilds in Dublin in 1840 when the guild system was dissolved (Clark and Refaussé, 1993). They included guilds with such diverse remits as the Guild of Merchants, Guild of Weavers, Guild of Goldsmiths, Guild of Barber Surgeons to the Guild of Printers, Stationers, Painter-Stainers and Cutlers. These guilds were responsible for ensuring quality and price control of each of their individual areas. Each member of a guild automatically became a freeman and was also entitled to vote in parliamentary elections.

There were two tiers within the corporation. The first was the common council which was where the guild's direct representatives sat. They debated and suggested changes and reforms which were passed to the higher board for consideration. Two high sheriffs were drawn from the common council. They served for a year and, like the mayor, were directly responsible for a number of law and justice tasks such as the empanelling of juries to try cases in city courts as well as managing prisoners, including their delivery to and from court and prison. They also processed and executed warrants for the arrest of debtors. High sheriffs presided over city executions and were responsible for maintaining law and order at these occasions (Henry, 1994: 20). They were, in effect, assistants to the Lord Mayor helping him carry out his duties.

The second, higher tier within the corporation was the board of aldermen, from which the mayor was elected. Throughout the medieval and early-modern period a large number of the men elected to the aldermen board, and subsequently to the office of Lord Mayor, came from the powerful and wealthy Merchants' Guild. Positions on the board of aldermen were held for life and, though unpaid, provided much opportunity for both social and business advancement. From the sixteenth century, new charters granted to Dublin enhanced the city's standing and increased the corporation's jurisdiction of powers. As David Dickson described it, this led to "a concentration of power among the wealthier merchants, the families from whom the aldermen were recruited" (2014: 35). These changes also resulted in an "increased social distance between the board of twenty-four aldermen chaired by the mayor, which met every Friday, and the Commons made up of younger merchants and spokesmen for the other guilds, which met once a quarter" (2014: 35). Representatives on the common council were separated at meetings from the aldermen, holding their meetings at the same time but in different rooms within the city Tholsel, a building which was also used by those guilds who did not have their own offices (highlighting further the close connection between these bodies).[4]

Until the Corporation Reform Act of 1760, entitled the 'Act for better regulating the corporation of the city of Dublin', the board of aldermen elected their own members (Hill, 1997: 128-129). After this legislation, the common council suggested members for election, thereby breaking up the dominance on the board of the merchant's guild, and of particular families. While the office of Lord Mayor was held by members of the alderman board, no alderman could hold the position twice. However, during periods when there was a shortage of people who could serve in the office, like the reformation (when Catholics refused to hold an office that was now reserved for Protestants) or war times, it was common for aldermen to hold the office more than once. Elections were held each year for the position of mayor, but it was usual that the longest serving alderman who had not already held the post would be chosen.

As the role of mayor of Dublin evolved from the thirteenth century, the serving alderman became responsible for an increasing number of financial, judicial and administrative duties. These functions can be divided into several areas: head of the corporation and guilds, chief magistrate overseeing order, and justice of the city. As head of the corporation and guilds the mayor presided over, called, chaired and dismissed corporation assemblies; appointed members to committees; and swore in freemen to the guilds and to new positions in the corporation. As chief magistrate he was also responsible for overseeing the city market places which fell under the jurisdiction of Dublin Corporation. This included regulating weights and measures in the markets; regulating prices during times of scarcity or famine; and fining traders for breaking rules. He was also to punish those who caused trouble in the market house and had the right to enter any market, shop or warehouse to ensure that goods were of an adequate standard (Hill, 2001: 150). Disputes arising in the markets were to be resolved by the Lord Mayor or under his direction. If he was displeased with produce, then he was responsible for penalizing the trader and he was expected 'to seize, burn or publicly destroy' the goods.[5] The Lord

---

[4] While Dublin no longer has a Tholsel, the building has a long history in the city with the first Tholsel dating back as far as the thirteenth century and being described as "a common house for executing laws" (Dickson, 2014: 35).

[5] Freeman's Journal, 24th September 1763.

Mayor also played a significant role in justice and the maintenance of order in the city. He oversaw the punishment of groups or individuals who disrupted the peace of the city and, along with the High Sheriffs, presided over executions. He also provided licences for plays and theatre productions within the city limits. As the office was unpaid, the diligence with which individual lord mayors undertook these duties could vary widely. It was difficult for them to step away from their businesses for a year to fully devote to the many duties attached to the office.

An additional, and not unimportant, duty of the serving Lord Mayor was to reflect the importance and dignity of the city of Dublin. This was done in a number of ways, including the holding of ceremonies over which the lord mayor presided, the hosting of large social and civic gatherings by the lord mayor and through the wealthy and powerful people who took up the office. The importance of the office was reaffirmed every three years through the ceremony of riding the franchises "when the mayor, accompanied by four hundred citizens on horseback rode around the boundaries of the city" (Clark and Refaussé, 1993: 12-13). Members of the merchants' guild, the most powerful guild in the city because of their financial importance, followed directly behind the Lord Mayor highlighting his own rank. They were followed in the procession by the other guilds. The flamboyant ceremony highlighted the status of the Lord Mayor, but also demonstrated the strength and power of the guilds, displaying their ancient lineages, strength of numbers and the overall guild hierarchy.[6]

Dublin's mayor would have hosted numerous social occasions throughout his term of office. Richard Stanyhurst's *Description of Ireland* written in the sixteenth century included a description of this socialising while in office: "There hath been of late years a worshipful gentleman, named Patrick Sarsfield, that bare the office of mayoralty in Dublin, who kept so great port in this year [1577], as his hospitality [has] led] to his fame and renown" (Pakenham and Pakenham 1988: 307).[7] He added that during Sarsfield's term of office "his house was so open,

---

[6] The ceremony also awarded freedom or the thanks of the guilds to individuals within the city whom they collectively felt had made reforms which protected the rights of the citizens or encouraged trade.

[7] This was included in Holinshed's *Chronicles of England, Scotland, and Ireland* "a playne and perfecte description" of Ireland.

as commonly from five of the clock in the morning, to ten at night" and all who visited were fed (*ibid.*). As the office was unpaid for most of its history, a small stipend was provided to the mayor to specifically cover the costs of entertaining. Nevertheless, this stipend rarely seemed to cover the actual cost of socialising and there were numerous petitions for the remuneration to be increased (McManus and Griffith, 2013: 24). By the eighteenth century, these social occasions had become quite elaborate. At the close of John Darragh's term in 1782 he held a ball at the Mansion House which included fireworks. It was reported that "the bowling green [of the Mansion House] was lighted in a superb manner, the supper was elegant and the whole did honour to the entertainer" (Dublin Journal, 1782). Nine years later at the opening of Henry Gore Sankey's term in office in 1791 he held a large dinner at the Mansion House and provided a turtle for his guests that reportedly weighed 179 pounds. The lord lieutenant attended and sat at the right hand of the mayor (Dublin Journal, 1791a). Taking up the office of Lord Mayor allowed Dublin's commercial elite to socialise with Ireland's upper class and opened up connections for them that their tradesman status would not normally have allowed for.

While the office could be an expensive one to maintain there were also many perks and privileges that could be enjoyed by the office holder. From 1715 the Lord Mayor took up residence in the Mansion House on Dawson Street. This house had been purchased from Joshua Dawson for £3,500, including an agreement that Dawson built an adjoining large reception room for civic receptions. It became known as the Oak Room and continues to serve this purpose to the present day (Clark, 2015: 17). The first Lord Mayor to take up residence was John Stoyte who lived there during his term 1715-1716. The residence did not become known as the Mansion House until 1776, being variously called the Lord Mayor's House and the Mayoralty House (Clark, 2015: 18-19). In addition to residence in the Mansion House, the mayor was provided with a state coach from 1791. Henry Gore Sankey was the first Lord Mayor to ride in the new State Coach, a highly publicised occasion where the carriage was acclaimed for presenting the chief magistrate "with splendour proportionate to his rank and authority" (Dublin Journal, 1791b).[8] It is noteworthy that the occasion for the

---

[8] A coach for the lord mayor had been commissioned since 1763 but this commission was never carried out (Dublin Journal, 1763). In July 1789 a

coach's first use was the annual celebration of the birth and landing of William of Orange (4th November) when traditionally a cavalcade of civic and national figures went in state to Dublin castle. Such a ceremony highlights the political complexion of the office of Lord Mayor and the on-going ties between civic and national politics.

The Lord Mayor may have been called Dublin's first citizen but the office was overshadowed by government in Dublin Castle and the parliament. As the capital was the residence of many national leaders, and the government administration, as well as the Irish gentry, the running of the city was a topic of great interest to these powerful bodies. From the creation of the office of Lord Mayor, the office was at risk of being dominated by national government. Dublin Castle was operational as a base for English government in Ireland by 1230 and it evolved alongside Dublin Corporation. This meant that throughout the long history of the office in Ireland, the city's mayor (although technically the first citizen of Dublin) was surpassed in power and importance by the Viceroy, Chief Secretary, Lord Lieutenant or serving equivalent at Dublin Castle, and from the late seventeenth century the MPs sitting at College Green. It also meant that national politics would always have a great influence over the office of Lord Mayor and corporation and over the city of Dublin.

The influence of national government over local government became most pronounced during the reformation when the corporation and guilds had to conform to the established church to remain in office. This led to much friction not just within the corporation but for prominent civic families. In 1580 Margaret Ball, who refused to conform to the new Church of Ireland, was arrested by the serving Lord Mayor of Dublin, Walter Ball, who was also her son. He had his mother and her chaplain imprisoned in Dublin Castle. Margaret died there and became one of the first Irish martyrs of the reformation (Lennon, 1989: 156-157). Religion continued to be a major point of contention between national and local government.

Lennon suggests that "by 1613 Religion had become the major point at issue between the royal administration and the majority of the

---

proposal was put to the Corporation and accepted that, at the cost of £600, a state coach be commissioned for the use of the Lord Mayor *Calendar of Ancient Records of Dublin*, v. xiv, 114-5. The eventual cost far outstripped the proposed price with the bill standing at £2,690 13s 5d on its completion (Bennett, 1994: 124).

Dublin Civic leaders" (1989: 207). While there were other issues such as finance and trading monopolies "confessional dissent on the part of the patriciate was fundamental to the members' extrusion from municipal power within a generation" (Lennon, 1989: 207). Dublin's commercial communities responded with a kind of religious flexibility that would allow them to hold office when the opportunity presented itself. From the early seventeenth century, the English government attempted to assert its control over Ireland and eradicate the Catholic religion. It targeted the corporation where it "aimed to erode the power and privileges of the civic elite and, more significantly, to exclude Catholics from positions of power and replace with a Protestant and increasingly English, civic government" (Stapleton, 2013: 44). From the seventeenth century onwards, particularly in light of the 1641 rebellion and the Glorious Revolution of 1690, it became untenable for the corporation to elect any mayor who did not adhere to the Church of Ireland. This was upheld by the Oath of Supremacy which every serving Lord Mayor was required to take.

The prohibition on Catholics serving in the office of Lord Mayor, and in positions throughout the corporation continued through the eighteenth century. Catholics were allowed the title of 'quarter-brother' in guilds although many refused to take this up as it gave them no say in the guilds and did not allow them access to the corporation itself. Catholics simply traded outside the confines of these organisations and did so quite successfully (Hill, 1997: 210). Nevertheless, they were denied a voice and were unable to influence commercial and civic policy. Guild members were freemen which meant they could vote in national elections, another privilege denied to Catholics. Jacqueline Hill who has investigated the civic life of Dublin in this period says that 'the door' to public life "had been kept firmly closed for Catholics" (Hill, 1997: 195). Nevertheless, the proportion of Protestants in the population of the city was decreasing in this period and Catholics were numerically dominant. While the city's population stood at 180,000 in 1798, it is estimated that just 30 per cent were Protestant (Hill, 1997: 197). The tide was turning and from the 1770s there were a number of relief acts of which Catholics could take advantage. Under a 1793 relief bill, for example, Catholics were granted entrance to civic institutions, although in practice the guilds still controlled who they let in. When the merchants' guild met to swear in new members in July 1793, the guild showed their distaste for the relief act by rejecting two of the

16

city's most powerful Catholic merchants, Edward Byrne and Valentine O'Connor (Dublin Journal/Saunder's Newsletter, 1793). Catholics fared better when the corporation met on 18 October to admit new members to the freedom of the city. "Of more than twenty petitions for freedom of persons professing popish religion, but *one* (that of Mr. V. O'Connor) was sent down from the board of Aldermen, which was upon ballot *rejected* in the commons by 66 against 29" (The Dublin Journal/Saunder's Newsletter, 1793). O'Connor had been one of the prominent agitator's in gaining the relief, so his exclusion was a clear message to Catholics that the guilds could, and would, vote in who they liked. The Protestant hold on civic office was maintained even after Catholic Emancipation with one liberal Protestant contemporary, Lord Cloncurry, describing Irish corporations as "traders in religious intolerance" (Hill, 1997: 364). While municipal reform, spear-headed by Daniel O'Connell, was debated and attempted, it would take a parliamentary commission and the dissolution of the guilds in 1840 to truly open up the corporation membership, and the office of Lord Mayor, to Catholics (Clark, 2013: 107).

There were visible signs that the corporation's power and influence was in decline from the eighteenth century. Attempts by the corporation to maintain itself as a Protestant institution weakened it further and made it less relevant. Some of the earlier celebrations of the office had also disappeared by the nineteenth century. The Riding of the Franchises, where the Lord Mayor asserted the corporation's jurisdiction over the city boundaries, was last held in 1785. This event had descended into riot, with military intervention required to disperse the crowds; three people died in the incident (Dickson, 2014: 88).

During two corporation disputes in 1711 and 1790 which centred on the election of the Lord Mayor, the state, in the form of the privy council, had to intervene to bring pressure to bear to bring about a resolution. The Wide Street's Commissioners who undertook city improvements in the eighteenth and nineteenth century were appointed and led by parliament. The projects undertaken by the commission were far more ambitious than anything the corporation could resource and included opening-up access to Essex Bridge and alleviating traffic congestion, opening up Dame Street, broadening and widening of Sackville Street (now O'Connell Street) and the development of Westmoreland Street (Dickson, 2014: 225). This is just one example of how the corporation's remit was being reduced, and along with it the perceived power of the Lord Mayor.

From 1841, when the Municipal Corporation Reform Act came into effect, the two-tiered corporation was replaced by a new, more representative city council with councillors being directly elected by men who held property to the value of £10. These changes meant that a significant proportion of the Catholic population could now vote and it represented a revolution in terms of membership of the city's ruling council. The election of Daniel O'Connell as Lord Mayor in 1841 was a further indication that change had arrived (Clark, 2013: 109). In the following decades the council was more evenly balanced between Protestant and Catholic members and by the late nineteenth and early twentieth century's this diversity manifested itself in a nationalist and unionist divide within the city council, which reflected the wider political scene in Ireland. The 1898 Local Government Act invested increased powers in the office and this "led to greater public and press interest in Dublin city hall". One of the more progressive aspects of this act was that it widened the electorate and allowed women, as well as many other workers who were previously disenfranchised, to vote and "as a result the municipal electoral roll increased almost fourfold" (Wallace, 2013: 120). Although women were now entitled to vote in local elections, it would be more than forty years before Cllr. Kathleen Clarke, the first female Lord Mayor, took office (Litton, 2013: 166). She was followed just under twenty years later by Cllr. Catherine Byrne in 1958, while the third female Lord Mayor, Cllr. Carmencita Hederman, took office more than thirty years later in 1987, proving that the mayoralty was slow to adapt. As previously noted, only eight women have held the office to date.

Political intervention in the office of Lord Mayor and in the affairs of the city has not been confined to the period before Irish independence. On two separate occasions during the twentieth century, national government suspended the city council and with it the office of Lord Mayor. In the early years of the Free State the new government, who had long used city councils for promoting their nationalist cause, were unsure of the role of the city council. In 1924, for reasons which were never made clear, Dublin City Council was dissolved and the office of Lord Mayor was suspended. Dublin was governed for the next six years by three commissioners appointed by the minister for local government (Dickson, 2014: 474). While the office of Lord Mayor was restored in 1930 along with the city council at large, the position was not always a popular one with calls being made, over the following years, for its abolition. Often these have been little more than populist appeals based on ill-informed perceptions that the role and office is somehow 'alien' or 'British', due to its historic origins and associated regalia. Even the holder of the office has, at times, been less than comfortable with its historical baggage. Famously, Kathleen Clarke, first woman to hold the office, refused to wear the Lord Mayor's chain of office, unhappy with its association with King William III, and ordered the removal of a portrait of Queen Victoria from the entrance hall of the Mansion House. The government intervened once again in April 1969, when the Dublin Corporation was dissolved by the minister for local government because of its refusal to strike a rate. A new Corporation was not elected until 1974, and Dublin was without a Lord Mayor from 25th April 1969 until 28th June 1974. Despite such controversies and misgivings, however, the office of Lord Mayor of Dublin has survived many vicissitudes since 1665, while continuing to evolve to meet the demands of a growing population and a changing religious and political backdrop. Probably the greatest threat to face the office is that which has arisen since 2001, with increasing calls for a single, over-arching 'mayor' for the Greater Dublin Area, to be directly elected by the people and to hold significant executive powers. The position of the existing, largely ceremonial Lord Mayor of Dublin, and counterparts in the neighbouring council areas, would surely be compromised by such a development.

The perceived need for an executive mayor for the Dublin region reflects the long-standing problems which have arisen due to administrative fragmentation in the capital. Indeed, the debate over Dublin's governance is well over a century old. During the nineteenth century, independently-governed suburban townships including Pembroke, Rathmines, Dalkey, Clontarf and Drumcondra remained outside the control of the city authorities, providing separate services such as paving, lighting and water supply. The largely middle-class residents of these suburbs paid their local taxes (rates) to the township rather than to the city's Corporation, depriving the city of much-needed funding for the many services which were availed of by the greater urban area. Despite various recommendations to extend the city boundaries, in 1881, 1900 and 1926, fragmentation of urban government persisted, with the last of the townships finally being absorbed into the city area only in 1930. However, the extension of the boundaries at this point failed to resolve the many problems which were caused by the growth of the city into other areas which are separately organised and governed, including the eventual spill-over of Dublin's built-up area into adjacent areas of counties Kildare, Wicklow, Meath and Louth. This persistent issue has long been discussed, with proposals for some form of unitary authority to handle the needs of the Greater Dublin Area, providing greater cohesion in planning and service provision.[9]

In recent times, the proposals to streamline the urban government of the Greater Dublin Area have become intertwined with suggestions about changes in the role and function of the mayor. Commentators have observed the rise of the 'executive mayor' in other countries, particularly in the UK but also in the case of New York City, and argue that the introduction of this new office, with significant powers, would benefit the city greatly. Popular support for the concept in Ireland perhaps owes something to the cult of personality in Irish politics, and the appeal of having a strong individual – one with whom the public is on 'first name terms' - in the position. The allure of 'Boris' (Johnston) or 'Ken' (Livingstone) has resonances with the fondly-remembered 'Alfie' (Byrne), one of the most beloved of Dublin's Lord Mayors, who served a record-breaking nine consecutive terms of office (1930-39) and a further term from 1954-5. The creation of the high-profile office of Mayor of London, a directly elected individual with extensive power, in 2000 generated a wave of interest in the concept in Ireland generally, and in Dublin more specifically. Just one year later, the Local Government Act 2001, the most significant reform of local government in Ireland since the 1898 legislation which had replaced the old grand jury system, provided for directly elected mayors beginning at the 2004 local elections; the provision was subsequently repealed by a 2003 amendment. However, the idea of a directly elected mayor remained current and formed part of the government programme agreed in 2007 by the Fianna Fáil – Green coalition. A 2008 green paper proposed a directly elected mayor for Dublin at first, to be followed in other cities at a later date. In the following year, Minister John Gormley TD made a commitment to a Dublin mayor and subsequently proposed the first

[9] See the detailed discussion of urban governance in *Dublin 1930-1950: The Emergence of the Modern City* (Brady, 2014: 69-103).

such election to take place in October 2010. However, the necessary legislation to enable this to happen, the Local Government (Mayor and Regional Authority of Dublin) Bill 2010, lapsed on the dissolution of the Dáil in February 2011, having reached committee stage.

The general arguments in favour of the directly elected mayor point to the need for 'real political leadership' in Dublin. Such coherent leadership is not possible, it is suggested, in the context of four local authorities, four chief executives and 183 councillors, and where each of the four local authorities (Dublin City Council, Fingal County Council, Dún Laoghaire-Rathdown County Council and South Dublin County Council) changes mayors every 12 months. Business leaders, including Dublin Chamber of Commerce, favour the model of a directly elected mayor to lead all four local authority areas, which they believe would bring economic benefits and an enhanced international profile for the city (Dublin Chamber of Commerce, 2015).

Following the 2011 general election, the new Fine Gael – Labour coalition passed the Local Government Reform Act 2014 which made widespread changes to local government, including provision for a "Directly Elected Mayor for Dublin Metropolitan Area". The process leading to the creation of the office of Mayor was specified and included a number of stages, beginning with a forum comprising delegates from the councils of the four local authorities which constitute the Dublin metropolitan area who would agree a draft plan for the mayor's functions. Controversially however, the Minister included a provision that each of the four local authorities would firstly have to individually adopt a resolution in favour of putting the draft plan to a plebiscite. Although the combined total vote from the four councils was 98-19 in favour, the majority of Fingal councillors were opposed, and their veto power killed the proposal. This veto power was exercised by Fingal in March, on the basis that the 2014 Act did not provide enough detail about the role and powers of the mayor and so people would not have known what they were voting on had the issue gone to a local plebiscite or referendum in Dublin. Following this rejection, the Minister stated that the Government remained committed to the idea of a plebiscite for a directly elected mayor for Dublin.

What does the Lord Mayor think?
What position has been taken by the Lord Mayor of Dublin in this debate? Although the holder of the office changes annually, there

appears to have been a degree of consensus as to the importance of the proposed new executive mayor. In October 2011, then Lord Mayor, Cllr. Andrew Montague, called for a directly elected mayor with executive powers and a regional authority to "drive the urban and economic regeneration of the city", a call which was echoed by his successor, Cllr. Naoise Ó Muirí. Similarly, during his term of office in 2013, Cllr. Oisín Quinn claimed that there was widespread support for such a position in Dublin, while Cllr. Christy Burke, who was Lord Mayor in 2014, said that the directly elected mayor was "long overdue". Public opinion appears to favour the new office, although there seems to be a lack of clarity over the exact nature of the role and its implications for the long-established office of Lord Mayor. For example, when in July 2012, an online campaign was launched by the self-styled *Democratic Dublin* group, the calls were for a directly elected *lord* mayor demonstrating, at the least, some confusion in terminology. Nevertheless, a telephone poll conducted on behalf of the Labour Party in 2016 found that 74% of Dubliners were in favour of a directly elected mayor, although the details of what that position might entail are unclear. The perceived widespread popular support for a directly elected mayor was discussed by councillors from across the four Dublin area local authorities as part of a roundtable discussion hosted (somewhat ironically?) by the Dublin Lord Mayor at the Mansion House in late 2016. The politicians present at the meeting agreed that the issue needed to be revisited and informally agreed to hold a plebiscite on the issue to give Dublin voters their say.

The idea of a directly elected mayor for Dublin has become strongly fixed, to the extent that two competing private member's bills proposing the introduction of such an office were introduced in 2016. The Fianna Fáil Local Government Bill introduced by the party's Dublin spokesman, John Lahart TD, proposes a five-year term of office for the new mayor and envisages a plebiscite in May 2018 with the mayor being elected a year later as part of the 2019 local elections. Under this model, the mayor would have (as yet unspecified) executive powers and fulfil a co-ordinating role for the city in areas such as housing, tourism, arts and transport, while working alongside a directly elected assembly. A similarly speedy timeframe is proposed under the Green Party's Local Government (Mayor and Regional Authority of Dublin) Bill 2016. This is an updated version of their previously proposed 2010 Dublin Mayor Bill, which had established cross-party support and passed all stages in the Dáil. As a result, the Greens suggested that their bill could be enacted quickly and come into force in time for the 2019 election cycle. The office created would have powers to develop strategic policy for the city in the four areas of housing, land-use planning, transport and waste management, providing the necessary leadership to tackle the crises facing the city, according to the Green Party leader Eamon Ryan TD. The new mayor would have a co-ordinating and leadership role as head of a new regional authority, sitting above the existing four Dublin local authorities, and would work through and with existing local government structures under this proposal. At the time of writing, both bills have been postponed and it is unclear when the issue will resurface in Dáil Éireann.[10]

Conclusion

Despite the many discussions which have taken place over almost two decades, there remains a lack of clarity around the potential role of a directly-elected mayor of Dublin. The variety of models of directly elected mayors worldwide, with differing powers and influence, is rarely discussed, with an emphasis on the London experience. The international profile of this position has perhaps overshadowed the fact that many highly successful global cities do not have directly elected mayors. In the case of London, the mayor heads a 25-member elected assembly, while the existing 32 London borough councils and City of London Corporation continue to operate underneath this structure, much as has been proposed for Dublin. The Corporation of the City of London is headed by the Lord Mayor of London, a continuation of a ceremonial role which, like that of Dublin's Lord Mayor, has survived for centuries. Interestingly, despite the prominence of London's mayor, the general public in the UK is not enamoured with the concept of directly elected mayors. When mayoral referendums were held in ten UK cities in 2012, Bristol was the only city where the electorate supported the establishment of the office of mayor.

In a traditionally weak local government system such as prevails in Ireland, the benefits of introducing a directly elected mayor with

---

[10] See Oireachtas records from 23rd November 2016 http://oireachtasdebates. oireachtas.ie/debates%20authoring/debateswebpack.nsf/takes/dail20161123000 45?opendocument for details.

executive powers may be less than imagined. Without changes to local government powers and financing, the elected mayor might lack the power to make any appreciable difference to urban development in Dublin. The existing office of Lord Mayor, despite its limitations, may in fact remain a more significant force in the government of the city than recent discussions suggest. The office has proven its ability to weather many storms. Although the guilds and two-tiered corporation have long been abolished, the office of Lord Mayor has survived this and many other reforms. The suspension of the city council and office of Lord Mayor in the 1920s and again in the late 1960s can be regarded as a failure, because these offices were too deeply embedded in the governance of the city. It is difficult to tell if a reimagining of this historic office can fulfil the ambitions of those who are proposing it.

CHAPTER 3
MAYORAL GOVERNANCE AND THE CHALLENGES OF INSTITUTIONAL CHANGE

Deiric Ó Broin

Introduction

Directly elected mayors represent an interesting case study in public policy reform in Ireland. Every political party appears to be in favour of it, nearly every key city-oriented civil society stakeholder, including chambers of commerce and city promotion groups, see the introduction of directly elected mayors as part of the solution to the challenges facing cities as they work to compete against other cities, and yet it has not happened (O'Loughlin, 2016; Manning, 2016; O'Donoghue, 2017; McGee, 2017a). What is so problematic about the proposal that sees it stalled again and again? What is it about the Irish public policy framework that makes it resistant to such a reform? Is it representative of a broader resistance to institutional reform or perhaps an example of the blocking power of key vested interests in the broader Irish central and local government systems?

While some chapters address the advantages and potential drawbacks of adopting the directly elected mayoral governance model and examine the experience of countries that have recently adopted directly elected mayors, this chapter focuses on why Ireland, despite numerous analyses suggesting this approach as appropriate, has shown no alacrity in adopting it.

The chapter begins with a brief outline of the background to the broader debate about local government in Ireland, in particular the recent interest in directly elected mayors. The chapter then reviews the parameters of the debate, particularly the focus on cities and city regions rather than counties and examines a number of the key claims made for proponents of directly elected mayors. The chapter then briefly examines the political context in which the debate is taking place in Ireland and reviews the extent and nature of the opposition to the proposal. This is followed by a brief review of the likelihood of directly elected mayors being introduced into the Irish local governance system.

Directly Elected Mayors and Irish Public Policy

Local government in Ireland is highly centralised (Roche, 1982; Barrington, 1991; MacCarthaigh, 2009) and general subordination to central government has been a dominant theme since the foundation of the State in 1922. In particular, local authorities are very dependent on the centre for finance as they have limited revenue raising capabilities (Ó Broin and Waters, 2007) and while there have been some potentially significant changes in recent years, e.g. the introduction of the Residential Property Tax, the manner in which it has been implemented has not increased the autonomy of local authorities in any meaningful way.[11]

In addition, it is worth noting a peculiarity of the early Irish state and its leading politicians, i.e. its unusual attitude towards local government. Despite the fact that the new generation of Irish political leaders' primary experience of governing, if they had any, had been achieved through the recently democratised local government system. The response of the Minister for Local Government, Ernest Blythe TD, in 1923 to Macroom Rural District Council's threat to withhold the delivery of its services reflects a widely held view that local government was a distracting and potential anti-government nuisance:

> I am directed by Mr. Blythe to state that from his knowledge of the work done by Macroom District Council, he does not consider that any important public interests will suffer as a result of its refusal to function.

As a newly independent state the Cumann na nGaedheal government opted for a centralised state. Corcoran contends that decision was based on the not unfounded belief that "local authorities were corrupt

---

[11] MacCarthaigh (2009: 46-47) notes a critical difference between the Irish system and other categories of local government systems in Europe is the strong role played by central government in determining the functions and financial independence of local authorities. This factor, combined with weak political structures and an electoral system that incentivises national politicians to maintain detailed involvement and high profiles in their communities (at the expense of local politicians), has played an important role in inhibiting the development of local government as an alternative locus of power and influence.

and inefficient and to prevent those opposed to the Treaty using them as bases for opposition" (2009: 13).[12] In this context it is not surprising that robust legislative provisions were enacted to provide a constraining framework for local government in the new state. For example, the Local Government (Temporary Provisions) Act, 1923 and the Local Government Act, 1925 gave the government the necessary powers to dissolve Rural District Councils and extend central control to all local authorities. In addition local authorities were severely disrupted between 1919 and 1923. Many failed to hold meetings. Rates were not collected so services could not be funded, resulting in cutbacks and outsourcing. The period also saw the government using its powers to dissolve twenty local authorities and replace them with government-appointed commissioners (Haslam, 2003). Most of the commissioners were competent administrators, apolitical and amenable to central direction. While the displaced councillors were displeased, ratepayers were seen to welcome the commissioners because they managed the councils economically (Maguire, 1998).

From the outset the central government, no matter what party has been in power, has been reluctant to devolve any significant power to the local government system. In July 1923 Ernest Blythe warned the cabinet that the forthcoming local elections would give every "crank and impossibilist in the country a platform" (Walker, 2012: 9).[13] It was a suspicion that has retained its potency for nearly a century. Arguably the initial decision to limit local government autonomy was based on a sound rationale, i.e. during and after the War of Independence and Civil War the local government system lacked the capacity to deliver

---

[12] It is also worth noting the drafting process that led to the Constitution of the Irish Free State made only "incidental reference to local government" and the constitution committee favoured centralisation, "only one of the three drafts submitted recommended decentralised administration and regional autonomy" (Corcoran, 2013: 23). In this draft, Article 27 declared that the "state shall foster the ideal of decentralisation and regional autonomy" and the Dáil would "transmit to local representative assemblies such derivative authority in legislative, administrative, cultural and economic affairs, as is compatible with the unity and integrity of Ireland" (Cahillane, 2016: 33). The inclusion of a provision for subordinate legislatures had been specifically requested by Michael Collins.
[13] Blythe's views won the argument and local elections were deferred during the civil war by the Local Government (Postponement of Elections) Act 1922, the first of a number of deferrals before elections were held in 1925.

significant services or raise funds locally in a coherent and reputable manner. In support of this perspective Quinlivan argues that "strict, centralised control was deemed appropriate for a small, divided country with a new government seeking authority and respect" (2015b: 103). However it appears that the successor governments took a similar view about local government but the original rationale had morphed into a strongly held lack of regard for the benefits of local autonomy. The state had achieved a successful and peaceful transfer of power in 1932 (Kissane, 2001) and largely established a constitutionally-oriented and democratic political culture but devolution was not a component of this new dispensation and central government continued to provide a large portion of funding to the local government system, thereby reducing their financial autonomy, and "decided on accounting methods and maintained a veto over borrowings, appointments, salaries and pensions" (Corcoran, 2013: 43).[14]

The only significant institutional change to the system introduced in the Local Government (Ireland) Act, 1898 was the introduction of the local authority management system between 1929 and 1940.[15] The system was amended to address some concerns about balance of power between the manager and councillors in the mid-1950s but the dominant dynamic in centre-local relations is that local government cannot be entrusted with significant powers and powers that have been devolved are best managed by the centrally-appointed executive management as distinct from the locally-elected political leadership.

The Irish local government system is nominally based on the classical separation of powers, where the councillors have responsibility for reserved functions, i.e. they formulate the policy framework for the local authority, this description is rather misleading. Irish local government legislation states that all functions which are not stated in law as being reserved functions are automatically deemed

---

[14] It is worth noting that this centralised system of financial management is no more transparent and a recent international review of the Irish local government system observed that the mechanism used "for allocating the Local Government Fund remains a mystery to practically everyone in the local government system" (Council of Europe, 2013).

[15] The Cork City Management Act became law in February 1929. The city management model was extended to Dublin in 1930, to Limerick in 1934 and to Waterford in 1939. In 1940 the County Management Act expanded the system throughout the twenty-six counties of the Republic.

executive functions and are the responsibility of the appointed city/county chief executive. In such an arrangement one would expect that the councillors formulate policy and the chief executive is responsible for implementation and the day-to-day running of the authority. The reality is rather different as the legal separation of powers is not operationalised in a coherent manner. The elected members will try to influence the chief executive with regard to executive decisions while it has long been recognised that the chief executive is the major initiator of policy (Collins, 1987; Sheehy, 2003; Quinlivan, 2008).[16] In addition central governments have, on occasion, removed functions from councillors and allocated them to the city/county chief executive, e.g. waste management.[17]

Within this system each local authority elects a mayor[18] on an annual basis from among its own members. It is usually the case that the position of mayor is agreed in advance as part of a pact between the main political parties. Kenny notes that the mayoralty "is rotated among party members with one taking the chair for a year at a time" (2004: 15). The office of mayor is largely a ceremonial one and the incumbent does not have any significant additional powers in comparison to the regular elected members.

As Quinlivan observes "… for the best part of forty years following the City and County Management (Amendment) Act, 1955, there was little scrutiny of the management system" (2015b: 106) and it was not

---

[16] Quinlivan (2008: 7-8) cites Lindblom's 'Mutual Adjustment Theory' to explain how this aspect of local government operates in Ireland, the elected members and the chief executive "co-ordinate with each other … without rules that fully describe their relations to each other" (Zimmerman, 2006: 197).

[17] Davies notes that during the "1990s it became clear that Ireland was facing a waste crisis with landfill sites rapidly reaching capacity" (2007: 53). Unfortunately local authorities appeared incapable of providing a local solution, "the crisis was not simply a technical one regarding the capacity of the state to dispose of waste; it was also a crisis of governance" (2007: 53). As a consequence of what many saw as a councillor-caused policy paralysis the Government introduced the Waste Management Act, 1996 which removed councillor input into the development and implementation of waste strategies.

[18] Dublin and Cork City Councils elect Lord Mayors and many county councils use the term Cathaoirleach (Chairperson) but the functions and roles are identical.

until 1996 that the balance of powers at local level was again analysed.[19] This process was continued by the Fianna Fáil-Progressive Democrats government in 1997 and, in time, became the Local Government Bill, 2000 and as such was published on 8th May 2000. It is worth noting that at the time, the Minister for Environment and Local Government, Noel Dempsey TD, had previously announced that the proposed legislation represented the "most radical shake-up of local government in the history of the state" (Brennock, 1999).

A critical component of the legislation was the provision for a directly elected mayor. Quinlivan (2000: 16-17) notes that:

> In local government circles the reaction to this proposal has been decidedly negative. On the very day that the bill was published, the members of Cork County Council passed a resolution calling on the minister to remove the proposal from the bill. The Local Authority Members' Association (LAMA), the General Council of County Councils (GCCC) and the Association of Municipal Authorities of Ireland (AMAI) have adopted a similar stance and, at the very least, are seeking an amendment whereby a person who has not served at least five years as an elected member of a local authority shall not qualify to be nominated for the chair of a council.

This provision was subsequently repealed after a very strong lobbying campaign from councillors and, interestingly, backbench TDs, "many of whom regarded it as depriving them of an opportunity to fill a much-coveted position from within the council chamber" (Kenny, 2003: 116).

Wollman notes that the "demand for the strengthening of political and administrative local leadership", in particular the direct election of mayors is a global movement (2008: 279). As noted earlier, the current debate is not the first attempt to establish directly elected mayors (McGee, 2016a). We have been here before, without success, in 2001-

---

[19] The government published its policy document *Better Local Government: A Programme for Change* in 1996.

2002, 2008-2010, 2012-2013 and most recently in 2016-2017 (O'Halloran and O'Regan, 2016; McGee 2017b)[20]. Why has success been so elusive?

Cities and City Regions not Counties (yet!)

As noted above the focus of the conference was on mayoral governance in the Dublin region. This particular approach raises challenges in Ireland as historically the sub-national system has been a county and city-based system of local government. The intermediate regional tier has been largely absent from policy discourse. The Buchanan Report (1969) was probably the first policy contribution to work to identify and address regional challenges, in particular its highlighting of the powerful role of cities (Walsh, 2014: 70) but it was confronted by a robust and organised county and county town opposition.[21]

> The Government must have been aware that for every centre like Sligo or Castlebar which welcomed its status in the recommendations there would be dozens of other towns which would hear their death knell in the *officialese* of the Report. We are told that not all the Buchanan Report will be accepted but indeed why should we take the directions of our own development from outsiders at all? Are towns like Ballina, Claremorris, Westport, Tuam to name but a few - going to accept the crumbs while a

---

[20] Fianna Fáil introduced the Local Government Reform (Amendment) (Directly Elected Mayor of Dublin) Bill in 2016, the Green Party also introduced the Local Government (Mayor and Regional Authority of Dublin) Bill in 2016. The Green Party's bill is a revised and updated version of the bill that had completed committee stage in December 2010. In June 2016 the Minister responsible for the policy area, Simon Coveney TD, announced he intended to resurrect plans for directly elected mayors in Dublin and other major urban centres during his term in office (McGee, 2016.)

[21] *Regional Studies in Ireland: an exercise in regional planning by the United Nations on behalf of the Irish Government*, more commonly known as the Buchanan Report, was a significant analysis of the regional dimension to economic planning which had largely been ignored since the foundation of the state. The report, prepared by Colin Buchanan, a British town planner, recommended a limited number of development centres throughout Ireland, which would have a minimum self-sustaining size. This became quite controversial as there were only 9 centres recommended: Dublin, Cork, Limerick-Shannon, Athlone, Drogheda, Dundalk, Galway, Sligo and Waterford.

selected few take the cake (*The Western People* cited by Daly [2006: 252]).

A challenge for the traditional Irish approach to economic and spatial planning is what Gordon and Buck (2005) contend is a renewed optimism about cities, in essence, "a shift from seeing them as essentially problematic residues of nineteenth-and early twentieth century ways of organising industrial economies towards the idea that they could again be exciting and creative places in which to live and work" (2005: 6). An important element of their contention is that the origins of this shift in thinking lie in social, economic and political changes necessitated by a "qualitatively different economic environment" *(ibid.)* rather than a change in thinking about the benefits of urban living or improvements in the economies of large cities. These changes are flagged by "repeated reference to the imperatives of (economic) competitiveness, (social) cohesion and (responsive) governance" *(ibid.)*. It is acknowledged that these changes are not specifically 'urban' and they are not necessarily linked to a resurgence of cities. However, it is argued that in this particular context, and taken together as a set, they have been understood as implying a much-increased importance for cities in securing "societal success" *(ibid.)*. This set of widely shared ideas about "the emergence of a new urban era in advanced economies" (Gordon and Buck, 2005: 5) relates to a number of pervasive forces in a globalised economy:

- Cities are seen as crucial to the achievement of competitiveness, social cohesion and responsive governance at a societal level;
- Competitiveness, cohesion and effective governance have become vital to the survival of cities, individually and collectively;
- This set of economic, social and political concerns is understood to be interdependent and mutually reinforcing, rather than competing values to be traded off against each other.

City regions have attracted considerable attention in developed economies over the course of the last 20 to 30 years. These combinations of an urban core or cores with a semi-urban and rural hinterland linked to the core by functional ties are becoming "increasingly regarded by certain scholars and policy makers as (a) the motors of economic activity in a globalised world, (b) the most adequate geographical units for the experimentation with and implementation of new modes of economic governance, and (c) more fundamentally, the ideal scale for public policy intervention" (Rodriguez-Rose, 2009: 50). However such an analysis poses significant problems for a sub-national governance system like Ireland's. How does a county-based system re-orient itself to a more fluid set of social, political and economic dynamics (see Callanan, 2017a), or phrased another way, the "typical messiness of urban governance?" (Cheshire *et al.*, 2014: 178).

An underlying premise of the conference and most of the contributions is that a mayoral (directly elected) model of governance is a very appropriate solution to the governance challenges faced by city regions. This is not to suggest that towns and counties should not have directly elected mayors but rather than if Ireland is to adopt the model, city regions, and in particular Dublin, are a useful place to start the process as the politico-cultural issues that make county identity in Ireland so important to acceptance of governance arrangements are likely to be less problematic.[22]

---

[22] For example, the Report of the Waterford Boundary Committee (2016) recommended that some of south Kilkenny switch to County Waterford. It was proposed that 5,500 people and 20,000 acres of south Kilkenny transfer to Waterford. Waterford City and County Council welcomed the publication of the report however Kilkenny County Council was unhappy with the proposal. A local Fianna Fáil TD in south Kilkenny Bobby Alyward ridiculed the proposal, while fellow Fianna Fáil TD John McGuinness said no one from Waterford or anywhere else would take "one inch of south Kilkenny". He also likened it to an act of war. Kilkenny County Council Chairperson Matt Doran said the whole process was skewed entirely towards the requirements of Waterford City. South Kilkenny Fine Gael TD John Paul Phelan threatened to resign his Dáil seat if the boundary change went ahead and said Fine Gael would lose significant support in south Kilkenny. The decades long issue has raised tensions on both sides of the county border, particularly in Ferrybank, which is divided between Waterford and Kilkenny (RTÉ, 2017). When a boundary committee was established in 2015 to review a proposed extension of Westmeath into Roscommon to reflect the expansion of Athlone, it received almost 28,000 objections from those wishing to protect the current Roscommon boundaries (Athlone Boundary Review Committee, 2016).

Main Claims for Directly Elected Mayors[23]

A key component of proposals to introduce directly elected mayors in Ireland has been the articulation of benefits the model would bring (Reid, 2004; Hyland, 2012; O'Donoghue, 2017; McGee 2017a). Previous research has reviewed the potential advantages and disadvantages of new models of governance for the Dublin region (Ó Broin and Jacobson, 2010) and to borrow Pike's phrase, there has been "a torrent of hype and hope" invested in many of the proposals for directly elected mayors as a governance fix (Pike, 2017). To date the local government system, despite some very significant changes over the past 20 years remains an outlier in comparison to our EU counterparts and the discussions about directly elected mayors, while welcome, have the potential to hide the necessity for a much broader discussion about local government, the role of management vis-à-vis elected councillors, financial autonomy, tax-raising powers, citizen involvement, enterprise and economic development. There is a danger that the introduction of directly elected mayors could be an *ad hoc* and piecemeal response to a much broader set of challenges for local government. While it might be overstating the situation to claim that the proposals for directly elected mayors are at risk of becoming "an article of faith rather than of fact" (Pike, 2017) there is a requirement for robust assessment of, and reflection on, the potential and perils of directly elected mayors to make the most of their emergence and not end up disappointed with a local government reform process again. The value relative to other potential reforms needs careful scrutiny.

In assessing the various proposals, it is important to recognise that there are different understandings and definitions of mayors internationally with different powers, responsibilities, resources and geographical remits. No single or universal type of mayor exists. This means we have to exercise caution in generalising from selective international evidence and muddling comparison of different systems and processes that happen to use similar terms.

Three main claims have been made for directly elected mayors in Ireland and internationally:

- Directly elected mayors will facilitate economic growth;
- Directly elected mayors will provide visible leadership;

---

[23] The framework for this analysis is based on Andy Pike's recent review of Metro-Mayors in England (Pike, 2017).

- Directly elected mayors will enhance local accountability and democratic engagement.

In the Dublin region, the first claim is strongly associated with the Dublin Chamber of Commerce (see Dublin Chamber of Commerce, 2015; Dublin Chamber of Commerce, 2017). The contention is that such mayors will be visible leaders able to make strategic choices on priorities, exercise power over policy levers and resources for areas including housing, skills and transport, and influence their partners in public agencies, the private sector and civil society. With a particular focus on city regions, directly elected mayors will be able to advance the economic integration and stimulate the agglomeration economies seen as central to city region economic growth. Yet this argument has not resolved the fundamental problem of isolating and attributing the role of governance institutions and policy in economic growth. It remains difficult to identify whether or not there is a causal relationship between forms of governance – including directly elected mayors – and economic growth. And, if there is one, what is its direction, extent, nature and magnitude? Do 'good' mayors generate economic growth? Or is it economic growth that creates the conditions for 'good' mayors? International evidence is mixed and inconclusive (Pike, 2017) and it demonstrates a *variety* of economic outcomes associated with a *variety* of governance arrangements. No convincing evidence supports the contention that directly elected mayors in particular and distinct from other forms of governance deliver increased economic growth and whether this growth will be of a more socially and spatially inclusive kind.

The second claim is that directly elected mayors will provide authoritative and visible leadership and cut through previously intractable policy problems. A single identifiable and accountable individual holding the mayoral office and wielding its powers and resources will have the mandate and authority to forge a clear strategic direction and carry along key policy partners and the wider citizenry. A clear leader will provide a powerful voice for their area in its dealings with central government and other actors in what Rhodes calls an "increasingly hollowed out local governance system" (1996: 652). To paraphrase Henry Kissinger's apocryphal question of "who do I call if I want to talk to Dublin?". It would be the directly elected mayor of the Dublin city region rather than four Chief Executives and three

Mayors/Cathaoirligh and one Lord Mayor holding office for 1 year terms. There is considerable evidence of charismatic and high-profile mayors that support this claim. However, the claim is problematic because of a lack of clarity on the definition, indicators and evidence for 'leadership'.[24] Too much reliance is placed upon selective, often anecdotal, stories of 'success' associated with mayors working in very different governance arrangements and contexts across the world. Too little attention is given to the negative effects of the concentration of political power in individuals and corruption cases which are also international.

There are considerable fears, sometimes articulated in a rather reactive manner, that the model of directly elected mayor suggested for Ireland is "somewhat lightweight" and likely to be constrained by the underpinning local authorities in the city region and unable to meaningfully navigate to the city region's advantage in the highly centralised Irish governance system (Pike, 2017). While there might well be lessons to be taken from international experience for the proposed directly elected mayors, the substance of such knowledge needs to be qualified and treated carefully rather than made a central rationale for this form of governance.

A third claim is that directly elected mayors will enhance local accountability and democratic engagement. In Dublin this claim was closely associated with the civil society campaigns to support the popular referendum in 2013, e.g. the *Let Dublin Vote* and *Mayor4Dublin* campaigns. At it most basic, the claim is that citizens will become re-engaged in the political process. The claim has two linked components. The first is that direct election of the mayor will improve the connection between the political leader and voters and be substantively different to the current situation where a large number of Dubliners don't know who their first citizen is. The second is that a closer and more visible relationship will be "forged between public policy outcomes and political decision-maker" (Pike, 2017). Unfortunately these claims are rather problematic. Fenwick and Elcock support the assertions and detail how directly elected mayors have taken "away old slow local government" (2014: 591). However it is not clear that such a

---

[24] Quinlivan's chapter in this volume includes a very pertinent example of an elected mayor, in a strong/authoritative model, fixing problems caused by his predecessor.

consequence is likely to occur in Ireland and mayoral elections in the UK, Germany and the US have significant declines in voter turnout, reducing the attractiveness of a key aspect of the model.

Questioning the claims does not reflect opposition to directly elected mayors in Ireland. Rather a concern that overestimating the impact of the proposal will undermine confidence in the need for further reforms. In the context of previous efforts to reform the local government system in Ireland, a key lesson is "take what's on offer, try and make it work, and push towards the next reform" (Pike, 2017). With this in mind the proposal for a directly elected mayor for the Dublin region raises important questions that we would do well to engage with: How will a mayor facilitate economic growth? How will the mayor exercise leadership and resolve troublesome policy problems? How will the mayor achieve higher voter turnout and greater accountability? And, lastly, how will the mayor demonstrate that a directly elected mayor delivers an improvement on other forms of local governance? Given the experience of our neighbours in England, the final question is more important than one might think, as the English experience shows a rather negative reaction to directly elected mayors and of the 12 cities to hold referendums in 2012, only one, Bristol voted to introduce the model.[25]

Opposing Directly Elected Mayors

This chapter contends that the obstacles to the development of a directly elected mayor model of governance, and a mayor with significant executive powers, are more considerable than is often accepted. As noted earlier no significant political stakeholder appears to oppose the idea of a directly elected mayor and some substantial political or policy proposals have been articulated and yet every major party when in government has failed to implement legislation.[26] Once in power governments have tended to "sidestep" the area and devise a solution they are fully aware is impossible to implement. The process of "sidestepping" occurs for a variety of reasons and this chapter contends that at national level in Ireland there are both politico-cultural and institutional reasons for this. This is not to suggest that political

---

[25] Birmingham, Bradford, Coventry, Leeds, Manchester, Newcastle-upon-Tyne, Nottingham, Sheffield and Wakefield voted no.

[26] O'Malley's chapter in this volume is unusual in that it is the first significant, coherent argument against directly elected mayoral governance in Ireland.

culture and institutions are separate. They are not. Political culture shapes the choice, design and operation of institutions of governance. In turn the institutions shape the evolving political culture. The contention of this chapter is that due to a variety of circumstances Ireland has found itself with a political culture and set of institutions of governance that mutually reinforce a lack of willingness and capacity to engage in a robust and meaningful debate about reformed institutions.

Coakley notes that in most societies the legal framework underpinning political life is critical but this framework does not exist in isolation. It is given life by the set of "political values and expectations that are dominant in the society within which it operates" (2011: 37). These attitudes are "fundamental, deeply held views on the state itself, on the rules of the political game and on the kind of principles that should underlie political decision making" (*ibid.*). This 'political culture' imposes informal constraints or freedoms on what is "politically acceptable behaviour" and defines the parameters of policy discourse (O'Malley, 2011: 114). As a result a state's political culture shapes how a state and society react to certain challenges. This chapter contends that Ireland's political culture and its interaction with the current institutional architecture of governance, in particular the nature of the linkages between the broader local government system and the key central institutions of funding, regulation and co-ordination, present very significant obstacles to efforts to introduce directly elected mayors.

Radical changes are very difficult to implement because "the political will to reform the aging Irish government system was weak and ineffectual" (Keogh, 2015: 3). These issues are raised not to condemn successive governments for their lack of appetite for institutional reform, but rather to build on a point made by MacCarthaigh (2012) that the Irish state tends to add layers of notional accountability and establish new offices or quasi-public agencies rather than interrogate whether the existing institutional architecture is fit for purpose.[27] This is particularly the case when it comes to genuinely addressing the challenges faced by cities and city regions.

---

[27] The recent establishment of the statutory-based Local Community Development Committees are an example of this tendency.

Why is this the case? Other research has detailed the challenges raised by climate change and the difficulties faced by Ireland in devising appropriate institutional responses (see Ó Broin and Kirby, 2015) and while there is some overlap in the root causes, the obstacles to meaningful local government reform, particularly the direct election of mayors, are distinct and require careful attention.

The first obstacle is the tendency to centralisation that now appears to be embedded in the Irish state's policy formulation processes and political discourses (Collins and Quinlivan, 2005; Callanan, 2003b). As noted earlier there is an argument that the challenges faced by governments in the 1920s necessitated a centralised response. However the initial response has become something more. It is now a clearly identified tendency, and, while acknowledging the "peculiar Irish context of economic and social changes" (Council of Europe, 2013: 12), Ireland stands out for its lack of regard for the widely held principle of subsidiarity.[28] Unfortunately, as MacCarthaigh notes local government in Ireland appears subject to "the continuing march toward increased central government regulation and oversight that has reduced local autonomy" (2009: 54).

The second obstacle is rooted in the apparently widespread lack of regard for the work of local government and those engaged in it within national policy formulation processes and key political stakeholders, including political parties. Blythe's comments in the 1920s were not isolated and reflect a problematic aspect of the local-national relationship.[29] It is unlikely to be as straightforward as "facing down the Custom House", as the former Lord Mayor of Dublin and Cathaoirleach of the Dublin Regional Authority, Cllr. Dermot Lacey

---

[28] According to the subsidiarity principle it is initially assumed that the lowest administrative entity, i.e. the local authority, has the competence to take a particular decision. Only when the next highest authority proves that a decision has an impact beyond the limits of one administrative tier should this authority assume the responsibility for taking it. The result is that decisions at all levels are taken as close to the citizen as possible and then politically endorsed in democratic elections (principle of democratic accountability).

[29] Ó Broin (2005: 82) found that many senior civil servants "didn't rate the calibre of councillor" and so designed mechanisms to exclude them from local development agencies and argued that "local government is the amateur tier of government, why would you ask these people to be involved in such a potentially complex task?"

phrases it, but he succinctly articulates a recurring issue for locally-elected councillors. The roles have become more and more constrained, new actors have appeared at local level, e.g. local development agencies, and bureaucratic requirements of the national department with responsibility for local government have increased considerably (Lacey, 2017: 6).

The third obstacle is linked to Ireland's preference for county boundary-based solutions to local and regional governance problems. The recent experience of developing appropriate governance frameworks for the Metropolitan Area Strategic Plans under the National Planning Framework (*Ireland 2040*) highlights the difficulties of building cross-county boundary governance arrangements. This is just the latest in a series of failed efforts to address county boundary issues. As Callanan (2018) points out this is a fraught process and reflects the deep politico-cultural attachment to county-based boundaries and their related identities and, just as importantly, the strongly embedded nature of counties in the institutional architecture of Ireland's public governance. In this context it is probably helpful for policy makers to view the Irish preference for county boundary-based solutions as an immovable object, in the political sense at least, and navigate around it. The result is likely to be sub-optimal but accepting it may lead to a constructive policy outcome, albeit less rational in the spatio-economic sense, but a positive outcome nonetheless.

The final obstacle to meaningful reform is the resistance of councillors, often unspoken, to a directly elected mayor. Yet, arguably their's is the most rational response in a local government system like Ireland's. The Irish local government system has the narrowest range of functions allocated to it among EU member states (Council of Europe, 2011: 50). In addition the balance of power between locally-elected councillors and centrally-appointed management is more skewed towards management than in any other system in the EU. In such a context a proposal for a directly elected mayor suggests that the mayor's power will mean a reduction in power and influence for councillors (Quinlivan, 2015b: 114).[30]

---

[30] Oonan (2017) outlines an opposition to a directly elected mayor for Dublin based on a combination of cost and an anti-local democracy platform. For example he suggests that instead of "wasting money on a referendum, not to mention the formation of another office, the Government would be better placed in investing the money back into all 31 local authorities. They badly

How can such obstacles be overcome and opposition be accommodated?

Conclusion

In many countries traditional approaches to local and regional government are being transformed. Long established practices and procedures are being questioned and "innovations in democratic and managerial practice now proliferate" (Hambleton, 2003: 147). Traditionally, there has been remarkable consistency to the office of mayor in Ireland, insofar as it has always been indirectly elected and subject to considerable constraints (Griffiths and McManus, 2013: 15). In giving serious consideration to breaking free from this consistency, Ireland is following an international trend.

It is not suggested that the British experience is perfect or even that it is one that should be emulated. For example, there are many with reservations over the UK government's belief that reducing the barriers to participation at elections and more direct engagement would encourage greater involvement. Could a revised local politics really inculcate the civic virtues on such a scale as to reverse the adverse cultural changes of the past decades? To expect it to do so may be to place an unrealistic burden on the otherwise sensible steps taken to improve the politics of local government. It is to confuse modest improvements in turnout with actual shifts in beliefs, motivations and outlook on political life.

It is this chapter's conclusion that we have missed a number of opportunities to:

---

need it". This follows from some of the arguments identified by Oisín Quinn. The second component of his opposition appears to be based on the lack of regard for the work of local government. While intimating a qualified support for local government the support is premised on an understanding of local government as the deliverer of services funded and directed by central government. The view that local government is an independent institution of public governance directed by local elected councillors, local political circumstances and local political choices, within certain accepted policy constraints, appears anathema. This understanding leads to a view that any move towards a directly elected mayor will, in reality, only facilitate central government absolving itself of responsibility for various policy failures, i.e. "let the government of the day off the hook, on critical issues such as housing, if it is able to pass the buck on to a single elected mayor figurehead".

- Expand the role of local government, particularly with regard to the idea of competitiveness and the key role cities and city regions play in globalised economic networks;
- Enhance, in an appreciable way, the role of councillors, particularly in the area of civic leadership;
- Embed a culture of citizen participation, despite the establishment of Strategic Policy Committees, Local Community Development Committees and Public Participation Networks, Ireland has been poor at establishing and embedding public participation in local policy formulation.

Further compounding these missed opportunities has been the lack of debate around the contributions Ireland's cities make. It is this lack of debate, as much as the obstacles to developing and consolidating institutional change, that will impact on any dramatic improvement in the extent to which citizens are empowered to decide how their cities should be run.

Directly elected mayors are not a panacea to all that ails local government in Ireland or a fix for the governance challenges of complex city regions. The introduction of mayoral governance will undoubtedly cause problems for the existing local political and executive management regimes. Mayoral elections provide opportunities for voters to rebel against established party machines. As such it will require a considerable leap of faith to introduce it but none of the problems, obstacles or challenges identified are a sufficient reason to avoid directly elected mayors. At worst citizens will be able to identify who is to blame and hold him/her accountable.

CHAPTER 4
A Practitioner's Perspective of the Efforts in 2013-2014 to Produce a Proposal for an Office of Directly Elected Mayor for Dublin

Oisín Quinn

Introduction

By 6.00 p.m. on Monday 31st March 2014 the councillors of Dublin City, South County Dublin and Dún Laoghaire-Rathdown had voted overwhelmingly by 92 to 3 in favour of the proposal for a directly elected mayor for Dublin. This proposal had been prepared by the forum of councillors from all four local authorities which I had convened at the request of the Minister in 2013. All that remained was for the councillors in Fingal County Council to vote in favour by a majority to then allow this proposal go to a vote of the public in Dublin. This vote had been provisionally earmarked for the 23rd May that year.

The level of support by that time on Monday was not surprising. Even though the councils were only weeks away from what were to be bitterly contested local elections there was an overwhelming mood in favour of allowing the public vote to happen.

The proposal from the forum had been painstakingly worked out following months of public consultation and many meetings, workshops and long nights hammering out the details. Every party and independents had been represented on the forum and each local authority had taken the opportunity to debate the proposal.

Throughout the latter half of 2013 the amount of public support for the proposal had consistently grown in surveys and polls. The survey carried out by the forum had showed that 78% were in favour of a directly elected mayor and this figure had strong support across all four local authority areas from both residents and businesses.

The feedback from the public was clear. Dubliners wanted clear, strong and accountable leadership to drive Dublin forward as a city in Europe. All of the feedback indicated that the current situation was simply not satisfactory. Decisions about transport, planning, on housing and investment to do with the Dublin region were being made by a multiplicity of agencies, local authorities, government departments and statutory bodies and even councillors complained that it was difficult to hold those who were making the decisions to account.

In many cases the system simply produced no decisions. By 2013 it was clear that Dublin already had a housing crisis and I had been compelled to privately convene a meeting of senior Labour ministers and councillors in the Mansion House to persuade government to take steps to reverse the proposed cut in the housing budget of Dublin City Council. A proposal to introduce a vacant site levy to compel owners of zoned landed needed for offices and residential development in the city was being stalled due to the lack of power in Dublin City Council to introduce the measure and a general resistance at national government level where outside of Dublin empty houses and offices was the problem.

The forum proposal was robust but balanced. It provided for an executive mayor with responsibility over areas such as transport, planning, housing, economic development and tourism. It was measured. It did not recommend the directly elected mayor having power over education, health or policing (other than community and traffic). It provided for the mayor to be accountable to an assembly of councillors drawn from all parties. The proposal would have required the mayor to lead from the centre, build consensus and work across parties. It would give Dubliners a clear say in the direction of their city and provide transparency and accountability as to how the person elected delivered on their programme. At government level there was relative silence although rising ministers like Leo Varadkar TD then Minister for Transport and Tourism had come out publically strongly in favour of the proposal.

But back on the evening of Monday 31st March the proposal was about to be killed and very quickly buried. That evening the councillors of Fingal voted. 16 voted against and only 6 voted in favour with 2 abstaining. Immediately in a statement released that evening the Minister for Environment and Local Government, Phil Hogan TD confirmed the plebiscite would not go ahead. In his statement he said it had been "necessary" to set a high bar for the proposal to be put to a public vote to ensure that there was "genuine political consensus" on the issue. He could not have been quicker to issue this statement that he "respected" the councillors' decision. The fact that across the four Dublin local authorities the councillors in total had voted 98 in favour to only 19 against was not, as far as he was concerned "consensus".

There would be no plebiscite and the first of the several hurdles contained in the Local Government Reform Act, 2014 had successfully repelled the momentum for change.

In this chapter I set out a practitioner's perspective of the work done in the later half of 2013 to convene a forum and to produce a proposal for a directly elected mayor for Dublin. Looking back on it now it is clear to me that - with considerable skill - experienced politicians and civil servants came together to make this effort doomed to fail. The stipulation that any one council could veto the holding of even a plebiscite is almost impossible to justify in the context of the government's stated agenda at the time of *Putting People First*. The plebiscite itself would not even automatically lead to reforms. Even under the Act it was not sufficient for a majority of each council to vote in favour of the proposal. The majority had to consist of "not less than half of the councillors". This meant that allowing for councillors who might not attend the meeting or abstain even more than a majority of those voting would be required. Even then, while the plebiscite was earmarked for 2014 the legislation only required the Minister to bring forward legislation to act on the decision within two years from that date i.e. by May, 2016. Given that the government in power at the time had been elected in the General Election of 25th February, 2011 this provision in itself meant the relevant Minister could run down the clock on bringing forward the necessary legislation even if the plebiscite was passed.

One of the first tasks I had when I became Lord Mayor in June, 2013 was to convene a Forum of councillors from the four local authorities. We set up a steering group consisting of the Lord Mayor and the Mayors/Cathaoirligh from each of the four local authorities and together we met with executive managers on the 11th July. Each local authority was asked to nominate councillors to the forum and our first meeting was held on the 24th July in South County Dublin. The forum then met five times concluding its business by the 10th December. In advance of each meeting our steering group met and we conducted workshops and laid the groundwork for the proposal. Experts prepared papers on the various different models of directly elected mayors from around the world. We used these examples of a basis for conducting public research and consultation on the various types of directly elected mayor. In addition to workshops there were public meetings, on street public consultation, social media debate, mainstream media and newspaper debate and various public surveys. The surveys were detailed and contained various options in line with the type of models applied elsewhere.

The feedback was strong and clear; and slowly but surely consensus began to be achieved on the forum. The public didn't want simply a figurehead, they wanted real reform. They wanted real accountability. They wanted transparency as to how decisions were being made. People were clearly ambitious for Dublin and frustrated at the slow pace of change in the City.

These demands were not driven by partisan political beliefs but based on people's experience of living in Dublin and living and visiting many other cities around Europe and the world. There was some tension and negativity on the forum at various times. It is no secret to say that most of this came from the Fingal camp. There was no hint in the public feedback of real people having an attachment to an identity of "Fingal". However it was clear that certain officials, public servants and councillors had such an attachment. Immediately concerns were expressed that this was some type of takeover by Dublin City Council. Painstaking efforts were made to try and persuade the members of the forum to keep an open mind on the proposal and to really listen to what the public were saying. In the end the forum's proposal was only voted against by one member of the twenty-two strong forum. However it was clear that the Fingal members on the forum intended to agitate on their own council against the proposal. I can particularly remember the statement made with some satisfaction by one of the Fingal executives that they had a veto. When I met with Minister Hogan to discuss my concerns about the form of the legislation (at that stage it was simply contained in the Local Government Reform Bill of 2013) I was met with the charming platitude that I would be well able to persuade the councillors at Fingal. I was subsequently privately told by a senior civil servant that many civil servants in the Customs House simply did not believe in local government in Ireland. They felt Ireland was too small for real local government and that local government was best administered by money being transferred to City and County Managers around the country to simply implement national policies. I realise now that I should have made a much greater effort to raise the matter with government politicians to have the Bill changed.

Our most productive meeting on the forum was the workshop that took place on Saturday the 9th November at the Mansion House. We worked through the proposal section by section. Relatively quickly we were able to reach agreement on the areas that should be transferred to the directly elected mayor's office. As well as the existing features of local government (planning, roads and traffic, community facilities, parks and playgrounds, waste, part responsibility for housing) the forum in response to the public feedback were keen to add transport, tourism and economic development. This would mean a transfer of staff and budget from various national agencies insofar as those agencies had responsibility for Dublin including the IDA, Enterprise Ireland, Fáilte Ireland and parts of the various transport agencies. By this time the Minister for Transport and Tourism Leo Varadkar TD had already come out in support of the proposal and had asked his department to go through all of its functions in a meaningful way with a view to seeing which could be transferred to the office of directly elected mayor. However his was a relatively lone voice at government level.

Councillors were also keen to ensure that the proposal was accompanied by reform of local government itself. In response to public feedback the mayor would be able to appoint members to a cabinet from outside politics. These executives however would be accountable to an assembly of councillors drawn from the four local authorities. The mayor's cabinet would have to be approved and vetted by this assembly and the annual budget approved by the assembly each year. In addition the assembly could by two-thirds majority impeach the mayor and the cabinet. Robust provisions for transparency as to how the mayor's office would work were contained in the forum proposals. In addition the mayor would have a strategic input for other areas affecting Dublin including education, health, policing and water but that executive responsibility for these areas should remain with national government and national bodies.

On funding the proposal was to create no new taxes but to provide that 100% of Dublin local property tax would be available for Dublin including a transfer of key staff and budget from various national agencies that heretofore had taken responsibility for Dublin. For example, when it came to promoting Dublin as a tourist destination Dublin City Council's budget at the time was significantly less than €1m, Fáilte Ireland's budget was well in excess of €100m although it was very difficult to ascertain how much of this was spent in promoting Dublin. In an age when people travel to cities or particular locations around Europe the argument for promoting a city internationally rather than just a country was simply unanswerable. On the transport side the lack of an integrated public transport system or integrating ticketing and the inexplicable delays in even moving towards these goals were continuously cited by members of the public as a source of frustration with the way Dublin was run.

Dublin vs Fingal

An issue that did not come up - but which we knew would come up down the road of this reform journey - was as to whether or not providing Dublin with the directly elected executive mayor would perhaps in some way disadvantage the rest of Ireland. All of the research made available to us was to the effect that Dublin was in fact competing with other European cities of similar scale such as Copenhagen, Edinburgh and Barcelona and that it was key to have a strong city competing on the European stage and that Ireland's only city of scale that could compete at that level was Dublin. In addition Dubliners were already paying more than half of the country's income tax and two-thirds of the country's business taxes and therefore providing for a thriving Dublin was only going to advantage the rest of Ireland in terms of national resources to assist with the national government's regional and rural development plans. These concerns however did not feature to any major degree during our discussions in the latter half of 2013. Rather, a bizarre concern about the potential effect of these proposals on "Fingal" began to creep into the discourse. The representatives from Fingal pointed to their lower commercial rates seemingly oblivious to the fact that the expansion of businesses into Fingal existed by virtue of its location in Dublin. Despite the fact that the city was the location of universities, hospitals and cultural institutions all of which were naturally enjoyed by Dubliners living in Fingal the argument was continuously made about the need to protect Fingal's budget. I remember joking to one of the Fingal councillors as to why they didn't start a movement for an Independent Republic of Fingal, to which he cleverly replied "Don't laugh, the airport is in Fingal!".

In one respect the proposal of the forum departed significantly from the majority view contained in the public feedback. The public had by a majority clearly selected a preference for the mayor to be accountable to a directly elected assembly for the whole of the Dublin region. The councillors on the forum largely were against this. In fairness they had a number of legitimate reasons. One view expressed was that a mayor could be elected on a popular mandate and his or her party could also sweep the assembly election thereby substantially neutralising the degree of accountability of the directly elected mayor. The proposal argued for by many councillors was to retain the four local authorities and allow those Councils to elect - using the group or D'Hondt system - to elect councillors from a range of all parties to the assembly. This would ensure that no one party could have control of the assembly. This would make the vetting of nominees to the mayor's cabinet and the assessment of the mayor's performance and budget much more genuinely vigorous. My own experience of being Lord Mayor on the Council and belonging to the biggest party (Labour) at the time but not one which had a majority was that this created the continuous need to discuss and test ideas across party divide with colleagues and to seek consensus. During the year I was Lord Mayor we were able to do this on three key issues: the budget (where we successfully came together to reverse cuts in particular to housing being proposed by the manager and central government); the proposal for the directly elected mayor where ultimately the members of Dublin City Council voted 50 to 0 in favour of the proposal and finally our policy initiatives on housing which were a product of cross party debate and discussion.

The forum also sought to ensure that powers would be delegated downwards to local area committees where those powers related strictly to local issues. There was a feeling that local area committees were often best placed to deal with exclusively local issues and should actually have clearly defined powers legally devolved to them. The forum recommended therefore that there would be more transparency about the powers and assigned budgets and that local area boundaries would be streamlined to reflect local urban towns and villages within Dublin. Many councillors felt that the representational role of councillors was important. Accordingly the forum recommended that while the directly elected mayor would largely focus on the executive responsibilities of that office that the four chairs of the local authorities could continue to represent the mayor at local events.

Despite the fact that this work was taking place in the run up to local elections, the councillors in the forum sought to work together genuinely to improve the proposal and to ensure that it could deliver real reform for Dublin in terms of its local and regional government.

The draft plan went through a number of iterations being tested in the forum and in workshops and being debated from a variety of different perspectives by councillors from all of the political parties and independent councillors. The true reflection of the merit of this proposal was the fact that it was supported overwhelmingly by three of the local authorities and across the Dublin region supported by 98 councillors with only 19 voting against.

In retrospect it is clear to me that there was a deliberate degree of coordination behind the scenes to ensure that Fingal County Council would veto the proposal for a plebiscite. That this was deliberately done demonstrates that the mantra in the government's national policy of reforming a local government to *Put People First* was simply a veneer to give the impression of a desire to change local government for Dublin. Stepping back, it should have been obvious that by creating an office of a strong directly elected mayor with clear executive functions over key areas that a major new political office outside of national government would be created and it is perhaps only inevitable therefore that there would be forces within national government that would resist this even at the expense of holding back Dublin's ability to grow which in turn holds back the country.

Conclusion

I still believe in this proposal as representing the best way forward for reform of local government in Dublin. I believe the big advantage of a plebiscite would be to create and generate public debate around the ideas contained in a proposal for a directly elected mayor with executive powers. This debate is only likely to improve and strengthen the proposal. The fact is that all public surveys carried out during the period of time when this proposal was being considered showed strong demand for the proposal. The vast majority of councillors in Dublin voted in favour of holding the plebiscite. There is almost no downside to the issue. In terms of the type of mayor that should be proposed I believe that the type of proposal which is in line with the public consultation is the best, namely, an executive mayor with robust powers who is publically accountable. Purely a representational mayor i.e. akin to a super Lord Mayor or alternatively a mayor who simply chairs at various committees representing the agencies who currently deliver services to Dublin) in my view would be likely to either be a waste of money or slow down decision making and therefore not worth it. In fact the research we carried out showed that the majority were not in favour of a purely representational mayor. Nor was there any significant support for a mayor who could not appoint his or her own team but simply had to work with the existing City and County Managers. Feedback indicated that this would simply make the mayor reliant on the City Manager/County Manager model. There was strong demand that the mayor be seen as being accountable and being able to bring outside professional expertise on a specific basis. Therefore I do think it is important that the mayor is accountable to an assembly. While the majority in public consultation were in favour of a directly elected assembly there is merit in the forum's proposal which provided for an assembly being drawn from a variety of different parties and would thereby require the directly elected mayor and his or her team to work to build a consensus and to govern from the centre. There is also scope in the proposals to give attention to additional reforms at local level such as having a small number of full time councillors who chair local areas or local urban villages in the Dublin region.

My personal view is that this change is vital to give the Dublin region the ability to grow to its potential and to be a major city on the European stage. This in turn will bring huge benefits to the national economy. Ireland needs a strong Dublin and a strong Dublin will help national finances which in turn will empower the government to assist with regional and rural development. Nonetheless a change such as this would involve the migration of significant decision making power and resources from a variety of national, statutory and public bodies in government departments and therefore it is important that it is the subject of robust scrutiny and debate.

CHAPTER 5
DIRECTLY ELECTED MAYORS: THE ENGLISH EXPERIENCE AND LESSONS IN WHAT NOT TO DO TO LOCAL POLITICAL LEADERSHIP

Colin Copus

Introduction

While the much talked about arrival of directly elected mayors into English local government is a relatively new political phenomenon and represents a mid-point in radical change in the way local political governance and leadership is structured and organised. The effectiveness of local political decision-making has been a long-standing concern for government inspired by inquires into local government (Maud, 1967; Widdicombe, 1986) and it was the Conservative Government of the 1990s that started to give serious expression to the possibility of directly elected mayors becoming a feature of local government (DoE, 1991; HMSO, 1993). Inquiries have focused their attention on, inter alia, a set of common themes: the transparency, accountability, visibility, legitimacy and responsiveness of local political leadership; the efficiency of local political decision-making; low levels of public awareness and engagement in local government and local politics; the intensity and impact of party politics in local government; the tensions between managing services and political representation; and, the tensions between representative democracy and public participation. Elected mayors are seen as a solution to these problems.

One of the main features of local government is the way it looks, Janus like, towards two often competing sets of processes and demands: first, there is a political world – and in English local government this is a party political world - of elected representatives, party politics, policy making, public and private discourse and debate, seeking party advantage and campaigning to secure a mandate from the local citizenry. The council provides the only local institutional setting for this party political and governing process. Secondly, there is the complex organisational arrangement for the delivery or oversight of public service provision which is driven by managerial and administrative concerns and which must respond to local priorities and meet national standards. Local political leaders and local governing systems need to be able to fulfil the demands of both directions and reconcile the competing tensions arising from political and managerial sources (Copus, 2010).

A key element of the debate about what local political leadership is and how it should be configured and conducted is focused on how citizens should choose their local political leaders: either directly at an authority-wide election or, indirectly by councillors of the majority party on the council (Leach and Wilson, 2000). Indeed, the debate cuts across Europe and has a particular resonance for those countries reviewing and reshaping the institutional arrangements for local political leadership, especially around city government as is taking place in Ireland at the moment (Denters et al., 2005; Berg and Rao, 2005; Rhodes and t'Hart, 2014). Currently, for the majority of councillors across England, one of their most treasured powers is the ability to choose the leader of the council and through that choice have an influence over the political and managerial direction of the council. The introduction of directly elected mayors means a transfer of power to select the local political leader from councillors to voters.

As well as the transfer of power there is a second central aspect to formulating the model of directly elected mayor and that is what powers the office should hold over and within the council and externally. An associated point to this question is what checks and balances should exist over mayoral power and action and where should the balance of power rest – with the mayor, the council or local citizens? It is in responding to these core issues in constructing the model of local political leadership that we can see how far the centre trusts the localities to govern effectively and how far both the centre and local political elites trust the citizens to select their local political leadership. As a result of the Local Government Act, 2000 which introduced elected mayors, there are now 16 such offices from a total of 352 councils across England (excluding the six metropolitan mayors elected for combined authorities in 2017). It is not therefore a model of local political leadership that has set England ablaze with enthusiasm.

The chapter will focus on some of the weaknesses in the model of mayoral government in England and the lack of powers and abilities that rest with the office. That lack of real power to govern a locality reflects the reluctance of the British centre to fully trust English local government and that trust is a pre-requisite of any fundamental change in the nature of mayoral power as they currently rest with English mayoral councils. There are two dimensions to the way mayoral government has been poorly formed in England, the powers held by the mayoral office and the power and functions held by mayoral councils. Those two dimensions are of particular importance to reformers in Ireland, seeking to restructure local political leadership, for without sufficient powers resting with mayors and their councils there is little to tempt either councillors or citizens into supporting a shift to direct election. Thus, the policy implications of getting the mayoral model correct, are clear.

The chapter explores the arguments that have led to the arrival of elected mayors into English local government and those maintained by opponents of that model of local leadership, to address straightforward questions: why do we have elected mayors and what should they be able to do? In addressing those questions the paper provides research evidence from 120 interviews with councillors on mayoral councils and with 9 of the 16 elected mayors in England (excluding the six metro-mayors elected in 2017). The next section briefly explores the roles and tasks and models of local political leadership to provide a framework for the discussion. The third section examines the debates about the merits or otherwise of introducing elected mayors and includes an analysis of the strength of party politics within this debate. The fourth section examines the weaknesses in the current way in which the office of elected mayor is configured in England and drawing on the discussion throughout the chapter suggests a new way of formulating the office of elected mayor to provide for a strong local political leadership able to respond to the policy problems and service delivery concerns of local government. The chapter concludes by indicating the responsibility central government has for ensuring the right powers rest with England's elected mayors.

Understanding Local Political Leadership

Local political leadership is a two-fold process of providing political direction to a council, community and citizens and of taking action to secure political objectives (Mouritzen and Svara, 2002: 52). Successful political action and political leaders' ability to bring about change to address complex problems at different spatial levels requires the leader to have appropriate tasks, roles powers and functions (Kotter and Lawrence, 1974; Svara, 1987; Stone, 1995; Rhodes and t'Hart, 2014). Without those factors in place the ability of the political leader to effect change is undermined and if taken alongside other factors which influence leadership style - psychological-personal, institutional factors, party organisation and systems, and political culture (John, 1997) then getting the balance between hard political powers – the power to enforce action - with soft political powers – the office from which to influence others - is crucial to the success of any organisational and political arrangement for local leadership (Burns, 1978; Stone, 1995; Elcock, 2001; Leach and Wilson , 2000).

In exploring how political leaders undertook their work Stone (1995) highlighted the need to look at what differences had occurred as a result of action taken and the way in which leaders overcame resistance, developed long-term strategic approaches to policy and governing, how they related to their own citizens and developed coalitions and alliances. Indeed, the latter factor is a vital way in which the local political leader can augment their soft power and influence where they lack the hard power to act (Boogers and Van Ostaaijen, 2009; Bochel and Bochel, 2010). Thus, much rests on the political skills of the leader or the support and resources that can be garnered to support political goals and action. In addition, local political leaders have to deal with 'events' and often unexpected political, social and economic events at that. Political leaders must be able to shape and lead events and use them to advance their own policies and objectives, rather than be a prisoner of those events. Leach and Wilson (2000: 32) describe this as a form of task orientation and as an indicator of whether a leader is likely to be pro-active displaying a clear personal agenda or be reactive and lacking any clear agenda for action. Council officials also act as a powerful influence on political leaders through advice, guidance, legal and financial knowledge and expertise, and organisational resources. Unless the local leader can reshape the organisation that is the council to suit their own objectives, they will be led by, rather than lead events (Leach, 2010). While political leaders are able to claim the public vote as a source of legitimacy they must also construct a purpose to holding office and develop their leader - follower relationships (Stone, 1995: 96).

Allowing for the personal qualities of local leaders adds an element to understanding the way they take political action and how that action can be organisationally supported by the council (Elcock, 2001; Elcock and Fenwick, 2007). Local political leaders require the skill to communicate and convince a range of audiences: national and regional politicians, civil servants, business leaders and public agencies (Lapuente, 2010) and also need the ability to interact with citizens in a small setting of political discussion and interaction (Bjorna and Aarsaether, 2009; Schaap *et al.*, 2009). Elcock and Fenwick (2007) highlight the importance to elected mayors specifically of both structure and agency as a way of examining the facets of the office and the way it is organised and structured, and the avenues for political interaction for the mayor both inside and outside the council and their own personal skills. What Elcock and Fenwick (2007) suggest is that the constitution of the office of elected mayor, that is the formal legal powers and responsibilities and how they are designed by – in the English case – by legislation and council constitutions (also a creature of central legislation) stress the importance of formal structure. Next is the informal agency of how the office and the office holder interact, create relationships with and devise a process for political exchanges inside the council. Indeed, for elected mayors interaction within complex governance networks external to the council and with a wide range of external public, private and third sector agencies has become an arena within which elected mayors can build coalitions which enable them to wield influence beyond the formal constraints of the office (Copus, 2006; Copus *et al.*, 2016). Finally, Elcock and Fenwick (2007) identify how the skills, personality, charisma and abilities of the mayor, that is individual agency, need to be assessed in understanding the effectiveness of the office of elected mayor.

The lessons that reformers of local political leadership can draw from the general outline of what we understand so far is the value of shaping and organising the particular office of elected mayor and distinguishing between individualised collective leadership systems – while also accepting that all leadership is collective (or collaborative) to some degree or another. What can be condensed from the above discussion in assessing how to construct a new political office that builds on the requirements of Irish local government is how to support effective political action by elected mayors and the importance of: structure of the office; powers (and the balance of hard and soft powers), tasks, functions and responsibilities; organisational support and degree of organisational leadership, control and resources; skills, abilities and qualities of the individual mayor; and, political resources available to the mayor – inside and outside of the council. One of England's directly elected mayors has commented in interview:

I'm not the mayor of the council; I'm the mayor of the borough and I have to get things done across the borough not just in the council. I don't have much trouble getting people to speak to me (other agencies and organisations) but then all I can do is press. There's no power where I need it beyond the council. I think Roosevelt said being President was a bully pulpit – well that pretty much sums up being mayor in the outside world.

The overriding issue, often missed from discussions about elected mayors, when it comes to constructing the new office, which reflects what the mayor above suggested, is how far does central government want elected mayors to be able to govern and how far will councillors tolerate power and responsibility being placed in the individual hands of the mayor and of citizens to choose the mayor. With the framework set out above in mind, it is time to review the debates around the virtue or otherwise of the elected mayor form of leadership in English local government to highlight the issues on which Irish reformers could do better.

Origins and Debates on the Merits of Directly Elected Mayors
The debate about the most appropriate form of local political decision-making and local political leadership has, for some 50 years, explored various options for reform, but within constrained boundaries. Those boundaries were set by the existing constitutional position, roles, tasks, functions and purpose of English local government within the British unitary governing system. Inquiries such as the Herbert Commission (1960), the Maud (1967), Redcliffe-Maud (1969), Bains (1972) and Widdicombe Committees' (1986) sought to reconcile the competing tensions between service delivery and management and the democratic and political role of local government, and devise appropriate structures within which they could be achieved. But the results of such centrally inspired inquiries shied away from radical reform and settled for revisions to the committee system.

In 1967 the Maud Committee recognised the failures of the committee system and the proliferation of committees which it saw as wasting time and causing delays and frustration by involving councillors in administrative detail (1967:35). The solution however, was to recommend the creation of a small management board consisting of five to nine councillors which would set the principle objectives for the authority, review progress, supervise the organisation of the authority, take decisions on behalf of the council which go beyond the then roles of officers and have responsibility for presenting business to the council. What Maud was suggesting was a cabinet in all but name (Maude, 1967: 41-42) but it stopped far short of recommending an elected mayor.

Almost twenty years later the Widdicombe Committee (1986) recognised the advantages of the type of management committee of members that Maud had proposed and shared its recognition of the need to strengthen local accountability and decision-making. Predating many of the criticisms of elected mayors as a system of political leadership Widdicombe was concerned about concentrating power in too few hands and demoting the position of those councillors outside the executive. Indeed, Widdicombe expressed concern at conflict arising between two separate governing bodies - mayor and council - and that decision and policy-making deadlock would occur, or that a political argument would develop locally about whether the mayor or council had the strongest mandate. The Widdicombe Committee conducted its research and produced its report against the backdrop of the 1980s mandate wars between local and central government. The Committee went further to criticise the personalisation of politics it saw as inherent in mayoral political leadership accepted in "countries with a presidential system" but which it claimed would be 'generally disliked in Great Britain'. Finally, the Committee expressed a concern that reflects the majoritarian and party controlled nature of English local government when it warned of different electoral cycles resulting in the mayor and council majority coming from a different party (HMSO, 1986, para: 5.26).

The reluctance to shift to a radical new form of local political leadership and government, expressed by these two influential inquires, was based on a number of factors: an adherence to collectivist local decision-making; a fear of concentrated power; the desire to avoid creating a powerful local politician that could confront central government; opposition from councillors; and, an unwillingness to disturb the role and power of national parties in local government. It was not until the 1990s that a clear argument for a shift to elected mayors began to be made with any confidence. That reluctance to embrace a new approach should not be replicated by reformers in Ireland or those attempting to stimulate a wide ranging debate about local governance. It is a sad fact that in unitary states the agreement of the centre is as vital, if not more, to secure change in local political leadership models and powers. The lesson from England is that official inquiries cannot be left alone to frame the debate and while they can provide a forum for the gathering of evidence and opinion and the exploration of options they may do little to shift received wisdom and the current policy status quo. But, some official impetus to the debate can provide a useful ally for reformers seeking to suggest more radical steps be taken.

A British government created working party which reported in 1991 (Department of the Environment) and in 1993 (HMSO) and the report of the independent Commission for Local Democracy (CLD) in 1995 started to make the case for the direct election of the mayor (or in the case of the 1993 report a core executive group of councillors). The then Secretary of State Michael Heseltine was (and still is) an enthusiastic supporter of directly elected mayors but was unable to convince the government to enforce change. Taken together the case for elected mayors began to be formulated on the basis that most local government in western Europe, at the time, was based on a form of separation of powers with the executive and council (or assembly) elected separately. Such a separation of powers, it was argued by reformers would overcome secrecy and opaque decision-making and provide for clearly identifiable local leadership so overcoming public confusion about responsibility for decisions and action; and, would stimulate greater voter interest in local government (DoE, 1991; CLD, 1995).

The debate about who should select the local political leader – the public or councillors – was given a spur by the election of the Labour Government in 1997 and the case was made even more strongly, and importantly by the government itself that direct election of the mayor would improve the transparency, accountability, visibility, legitimacy and responsiveness of local political leadership and provide it with greater scope to take action to solve local problems. Moreover, the Labour Government began to articulate an argument that saw political parties, or at least the activities of political party groups, in local government as a problem to be resolved and a major contributing factor to the secrecy and privacy of local leadership and decision-making. One of the Labour mayors elected in the first tranche of mayoral elections in 2002 and still in office, commented in interview:

> I argued in the party before and after the '97 election that elected mayors were right for local government. Once we were in government I kept pushing ministers and the PM. It was important they knew that it had some support in the party as the opposition to elected mayors was beginning to wake up at that time and we needed to move fast and be radical.

What became known as the Local Government Modernisation agenda of the Labour Government was set out in a number of publications, all of which assessed the problems government and local leadership faced and laid the ground work for the Local Government Act, 2000 which tentatively introduced elected mayors into English local government (Labour Party, 1995; Blair, 1998; DETR, 1998a; DETR 1998b; DETR, 1999). Indeed, it has been necessary to continue to present the arguments for change after the 2000 Act as the vast majority of councillors remained unconvinced of the merits of shifting to that approach to local leadership (DTLR, 2001; ODPM, 2004; ODPM 2005; Copus, 2006). A councillor interviewed after an unsuccessful mayoral referendum in 2016 commented:

> We argued, successfully, that it is too much power in one person's hands, that it's a dictatorship. There would be very little councillors could do and wouldn't be able to stop the mayor – we also pointed out anyone could get elected what if it was some maverick or UKIP or the BNP. We also pointed out how expensive it would be. People clearly saw sense and voted NO.

That comment sums up the pre and post 2000 Act position of those councillors opposed to elected mayors but, despite the arguments and almost forty years after the Maud Committee's deliberations, a local political executive became a reality for English local government through the Local Government Act, 2000. There is another lesson here for reformers in Ireland and that is to formulate some support at the centre, in Parliament and among civil servants, as well as among academics and policy think-tanks. There needs to be intellectual support as well as political support for a shift to elected mayors which can underpin government action and the political case the centre may want to make for itself. Prior to the Local Government Act, 2000 the modernisation agenda for local government, and the analysis of which that agenda was based, was set out in a number of key government publications: Local Democracy and Community Leadership (DETR, 1998a), Modern Local Government: In Touch with the People (DETR, 1998b), and Local Leadership: Local Choice (DETR, 1999). All of which were preceded by the Labour Party's own publication in 1995 of its local government proposals, which, as well as unsurprisingly setting out the terms of the debate that would follow in Government, also expressed willingness to see experimentations with the CLD's suggestions for elected mayors (Labour Party, 1995: 14).

Certain key assumptions underpinned the modernisation agenda as elucidated by the Labour Governments of Tony Blair: first, the need to separate the executive, representational and scrutiny roles of the councillor and to place them into different hands; secondly, that as councils and councillors were required to navigate complex and often chaotic governance networks of public, semi-public, third sector and private organisations and work in partnership with other public and private bodies, a clear source of legitimacy and local leadership was necessary (DETR, 1998a). Third, that political leadership and decision-making should be transparent, open, visible and responsive to citizen concerns (DETR, 1998b; DETR, 1999).

The committee system of political decision-making was found to fail on the assumptions of the modernising agenda as it was seen to be inefficient and opaque, "no basis for modern local government", and a "poor vehicle for developing and demonstrating community leadership: (DETR, 1998a: para 5.1 and para 5.7). Moreover, directly elected mayors would allow for a quicker and more legitimate response to the pressures local government faced from urbanisation, globalisation, Europeanisation, increasing demands on services and growing participatory pressure (Denters and Rose, 2005; Berg and Rao, 2005).

Political decision-making through committees, it was argued by the Labour Government's modernisers, clouded political responsibility and were anonymous and unaccountable and failed to "foster community leaders and leadership; and, local people had no direct say over their local leaders" (DETR, 1998a: para: 5.1). Political leadership, and the scrutiny of political leaders, needed to be a distinct and separate set of roles and processes requiring councillors to specialise in one or the other so as to produce: "greater clarity about who is responsible for decisions and who should be held to account for decisions" (DETR, 1998a: para 5.9). What can be seen here in this criticism of committees – which were at least open to the public and press, is a parallel criticism of the practices of political party groups in local government (Copus, 2004; Leach, 2006). That government criticism of party politics was crystallised, thus: "in most councils it is the political groups, meeting behind closed doors, which make the big and significant decisions" (DETR, 1998a: para 5.4). A challenge was levelled then at long-standing and well-established patterns of political behaviour amongst councillors. It was for these reasons that the government found itself "very attracted" to a strong executive directly elected mayor for the following reasons:

Such a mayor would be a highly visible figure. He or she would have been elected by the people rather than the council or party and would therefore focus attention outwards in the direction of the people rather than inwards towards fellow councillors. The mayor would be a strong political and community leader with whom the electorate could identify. Mayors will have to become well known to their electorate which could help increase interest in and understanding of local government (DETR, 1998a: para, 5.14).

The mantra of the modernising agenda for local political leadership became condensed into: openness, transparency, visibility, responsiveness and accountability and it was elected mayors who were to provide just that. Given the then government's certainty about the merits of elected mayors it might be surprising that the Local Government Act, 2000 fell far short of a radical overhaul of local political leadership. Rather, the government opted for voluntarism with a touch of compulsion – that is that the public could petition for a referendum on changing to a directly elected mayor and, on the receipt of a yes vote in that referendum, would then move to elect a mayor within six months. The lack of a total reform and a move to elected mayors across local government was down to one simple fact: the overwhelming opposition to it from councillors across the country and the unwillingness of the government to take on and alienate its troops in the localities.

A vital lesson here for those committed to reforming local political leadership in Ireland, is to play on government's usual lack of reluctance to pursue compulsory reform or change in local government. To do that there is a need to present the positive outcomes for central government from a move to elected mayors, to such an extent that they override the fears of party uprisings. Clear and accountable leadership, a direct link to the voters and a clear mandate to govern, present advantages for Irish local government, as it may prevent pre- and post local election horse trading and present the elected mayor as clear winner of a public vote.

A further area that Irish reformers may wish to improve upon given the English experience is the British central government's unwillingness to provide English mayors and mayoral councils with any powers beyond those already resting with local government or with the type of council which might adopt a mayor – county, district or borough. Currently, three English district councils have directly elected mayors (from a total of 16 mayors across the country, excluding the six combined authority mayors elected in 2017) and each of the mayors have reported their frustration that their relationships with the county council have not been strengthened, or changed by legislation as a result of the district council moving to an elected mayor form of governance. As a borough mayor commented in an interview, elaborating the point about the position of her council:

> It makes no difference to the county council whether I'm elected as the mayor or not; to them we are still a district council and they treat us the same as all the other districts. There needs to be some legal recognition that the district has an elected mayor and that provides an enhanced status and set of powers in relation to the county.

Despite this clear weakness in the way elected mayors in England have been configured in a two tier-system, the Blair government's enthusiasm for elected mayors was reflected by the Coalition Government of 2010-15 and David Cameron's Conservative Government of 2015-16. Indeed, the Coalition Government required England's 10 largest cities to hold referendum on elected mayors – only one of which, Bristol – returned a 'Yes' vote. The Conservative

Government also linked its devolution agenda and the creation of combined authorities, with significant budgets and powers over the public sector, to those combined authorities being headed by directly elected metro-mayors. The Cities and Local Government Devolution Act, 2016 states that, in order for a combined authority to take on additional powers to that granted when they were formed a metro mayor must be elected for the area.

Thus, we have seen demonstrated government support for elected mayors in local government and for elected mayors to head the new territorial configuration of local government, combined authorities. It is noticeable that the government has been more forceful in pursuing elected mayors for the new creations of combined authorities than in traditional local government. The reason for that is simple – the threat from direct election of the mayor to councillors is greater in the existing system where political behaviour are firmly established, political parties can guarantee continued dominance through private collective decision-making and where councillors, as influential party members have been able to mount effective resistance to government plans for elected mayors (Orr, 2004; Fenwick and Elcock, 2014). The lesson then is that the creation of new systems or configurations of territorial governance poses less of a threat to established political elites and so, for example those seeking to reform local government in the City and County of Cork, for example, may make the introduction of a directly elected mayor a condition of creating a new local government model for Cork. Resistance may however still arise, even when new models of territorial government are being proposed and in England some devolution deals have collapsed because of the government's insistence on elected mayors and combined authority constitutions were often designed by councillors to hobble the mayor once elected. The arguments levelled by councillor opponents of the model of elected mayor which take the shape of a series of myths about the office, can be summarised thus: concentration of power; accountability; corruption; and expense. The first objection – the concentration of power – holds that it is politically wrong to focus all power in one set of hands and those who employ this argument often greatly inflate the real power of elected mayors into almost dictatorial government.

A councillor sitting on a mayoral authority made the following comment during the research which encapsulates the objections heard from those councillors opposed to mayoral local political leadership:

With committees all councillors can have a say in policy-making and decisions but with elected mayors councillors have no say – everything rests with the mayor. It's un-democratic to exclude councillors and to concentrate power; we might as well do away with councillors – the mayor makes all the decisions and can do whatever he likes. Scrutiny can't and doesn't stop anything; the mayor can ignore us. Yes he comes under scrutiny but all we can do is ask questions. Even in the group meeting we can't really do anything if we don't like what the mayor has done or is thinking of doing.

The argument that the mayoral office is all powerful however, ignores the checks and balances through the scrutiny system and that the powers that rest with the mayor are broadly similar to those that rest with council leaders, chosen by councillors. A mayor's budget can only be overturned on a two-thirds majority (as has happened in North Tyneside and Hartlepool) whereas a council leader's budget (or in reality the budget of the ruling group) can be overturned by a single vote. The likelihood of a ruling group's budget being overturned is remote given party group discipline, but it is a possibility. Elected mayors and council leaders each appoint their own cabinets. It is the internal politics of a council and the personal skills and activities of the holders of political offices that makes the mayor or leader powerful rather than just the office itself.

The issue of accountability is linked to that of power and the mechanisms for accountability within English local government primarily and formally occurs through the overview and scrutiny system of committees. These committees are charged with holding the executive – mayor or leader and their cabinet – to account and:

- Consider and investigate broad policy issues and report to the executive or council;
- Consider the budget plans, proposed policy framework and other plans and make reports to the executive or council; including recommendations proposing amendments, to the executive or council as appropriate;
- Provide advice to, and review the decisions of, the executive and how it is implementing council policy;

- Make reports and recommendations, including proposals for changes to policies or practices, to the executive or council as appropriate (DETR, 1999).

Those scrutiny responsibilities apply equally to mayoral and leader cabinets and are the prime formal mechanism for accountability of both executive systems. Informally, within the council and particularly the party group, but also by individual councillors, the mayor and leader are subject to challenge, question and criticism and pressure to change decisions or develop particular policy options. That process is no different for mayor or leader – except the leader (chosen by councillors) may be more susceptible to this type of pressure because of the electoral constituency: councillors. Indeed, elected mayors have been seen as a solution to the lack of accountability of local political leadership and were favoured by the Blair, Cameron and May governments as a means of strengthening accountability through direct election by the public. An English elected mayor expressed his frustration when he commented in interview:

> I would love someone to scrutinise me; I wish scrutiny was up to the job. But, many of my lot (party councillors) will only challenge in the group meeting and the opposition just play silly games at scrutiny meetings.

Third in the arguments set out by opponents of elected mayors is the issue of corruption. It is a constant theme of opposition arguments that elected mayors are somehow more corrupt or corruptible than council leaders. Indeed, in thinly veiled racist terms, US elected mayors are held up as endemically corrupt - ignoring that not all mayors in the US are directly elected and also ignoring that councils such as Doncaster as a result of what became known as the Donnygate scandal, moved to an elected mayor because of corruption, arrests and imprisonment among the then council Labour membership (Wainwright, 2002). Strange then that opponents of elected mayors so concerned about corruption support a system of indirectly elected council leaders that allowed such corruption to emerge. Corruption is not a result of any new governing system, rather a result of a culture and the behaviour of individuals in any position of power (Anderson and Tverdova, 2003; Bergh et al., 2016).

Finally, the issue of the expense of the mayoral office and in particular mayoral salaries are raised by opponents to indicate that the cost of the direct election of the mayor is not worth the benefits that may flow from that system. While grossly inflated claims are often made for mayoral salaries and opponents of elected mayors in referendum campaign have often conflated mayoral salary costs with the costs of an election to produce a seemingly annual cost of having an elected mayor one thing remains the case: mayoral salaries are subject to the same independent review panel which recommends a salary level which must then be agreed by the full council. Despite claims by opponents to the contrary – elected mayors do not set their own salary level. It is the case however, that on average directly elected mayors are paid a higher salary than the allowances received by council leaders.

In one notable case the mayor of Doncaster only took a salary of £30,000 which at the time (2009) was lower than some council leaders' allowances. In 2012-13 the leader of Manchester City Councils total allowances came to just under £56,000; in 2013 the elected mayor of North Tyneside agreed to reduce her salary from £61,000 by £10,000 to just over £50,000. But, it would be fair to argue that given the role of the elected mayor some differential in salaries with council leaders is acceptable. The issue is really related to a broader question of how much do we want to pay our politicians of any sort and the answer in England is always: not much at all.

So, the arguments for and against elected mayors can be condensed into a set of political positions which relate to broad political concepts and practical political processes and it is here that reformers in Ireland must start to level a challenge. First, conceptually supporters of elected mayors argue that direct election enhances accountability, openness and transparency and ensures that the voter can clearly identify the local political leader. Sweeting and Hambleton (2016) found that the proportion of Bristol residents who say that the city has visible leadership had grown from 24% to 69% since the introduction of an elected mayor; in a small survey by the Institute for Government (2012) the proportion of respondents who could correctly name the Leader of their own council were as follows: 85% said they could not name council leader, 8% named the leader correctly and 7% were incorrect. But, the concept is that direct election strengthens the link between voter and political leader and as a consequence of heightening visibility also enhances accountability as voters know who is responsible for political decisions. Further, that such a link created by direct election will make the political leader more open and responsive to the views of the voters, unlike an indirectly elected leader who is more focused on the views of the party group of councillors (Copus, 2006).

Secondly, when it comes to practical political processes an elected mayor is freed from control by the party group of councillors (or can develop a relationship with the group that suits the mayor's own choice of political room for manoeuvre) and thus is able to take action quickly and based on a series of considerations – not just what the party group requires (Greasley and Stoker, 2008; Copus, 2011; Kukovic *et al.*, 2015). Freedom to act, for a local leader provides manoeuvrability, flexibility and enhanced speed of response – something local government is often perceived to be lacking. But, for councillors a loosening of control over the election of the political leader has direct political consequences as it means that political deals cannot be struck so easily, votes traded for cabinet or other council places, or dominance of one faction within the group decided by who gets a leader elected from their faction. It is difficult for reformers to compensate councillors for this loss of power but despite some rejection of devolution deals in some parts of England there are now six metro-mayors where local control over devolved services, responsibilities and budgets has been shifted from Whitehall closer to local government. Enhancing the role, functions and powers of councils adopting an elected mayor and giving councillors a say in those new areas, is a vital component of building support for elected mayors.

Direct election of the mayor ushers in a more individualised decision-making dynamic but one which is linked to an assessment of the opinions of the voters not of a party group of councillors. Thus, for councillors a new dynamic of political action must be created which is either based on securing mayoral accountability, or seeking to influence a mayor in much the same way as a political leader would seek to influence outside interests (Sorensen and Torfing, 2005; Torfing et al., 2009). Councillors are required to negotiate, compromise, bargain, develop cross party alliances on single issues, or alliances with the mayor on single issues – rather than expect to be able to directly influence what a political leader does through votes in a group meeting.

It is the loss of control over the choice of the local political leader by councillors, which is inherent in direct mayoral election, that is at the heart of all the objections to elected mayors levelled by councillors. Moreover, direct election of the mayor disturbs long-established patterns of political behaviour in English local government which are focused on the primacy of the political party group (Leach, 2006). Much of the other criticisms of direct election, made by opponents of directly elected mayors that have been considered above, are a smoke screen for a loss of councillor power and the threat to the primacy of the party group that elected mayors produce. But, as we have seen above, the powers of the elected mayor – at least in English local government – mean that councillors have little to fear about mayoral power. Indeed, the model of an elected mayor introduced into England requires radical reformulation to ensure that the office holds the powers required to enable mayors to meet the challenges of political action that they face. It is to that reform the chapter now turns.

Elected Mayors: Reforming the Reform to Re-energise Local Government

It is in examining what reforms are already needed to the office of elected mayor in England and when considering the fundamental weaknesses in that model, that reformers in Ireland can draw the most lessons. The contention in the chapter has been that far from being powerful local leaders able to shape the policy networks and policy relationships within their localities and be able to effect strong local political action, the English version of elected mayors lacks powerful features found among its overseas counter-parts. The point has been made that English elected mayors and mayoral councils have no additional powers over and above similar types of councils which use the indirectly elected leader system, or for that matter those councils using a committee system.

The legislative framework within which elected mayors operates provides for the sharing of certain powers and responsibilities with the rest of the council such as setting the council budget and deciding on certain policy documents, for example the following: Annual Library Plan, Crime and Disorder Reduction Strategy, Local Development Framework or the Youth Justice Plan – the council can, on a simple majority, insist the mayor revise and resubmit the plans; if the council wishes to see further revision or reject the plans, it must then garner a two-thirds majority. The mayor has responsibility for those other areas not specifically mentioned as shared with the council and on first glance this provides the mayor with considerable power. But, such decision-making is shared with the cabinet and does not extend beyond those powers resting with the leader and cabinet style of council. Both elected mayors and council leaders appoint their own cabinet of up to nine councillors. The Local Authorities (Elected Mayor and Mayor's Assistant) (England) Regulations 2002 gives the mayor power to appoint a single political advisor and set the terms of conditions of employment for that advisor. The sharing of powers does offend against the principle of a separation of powers and a model based on a clear separation – with the mayor deciding and the council holding to account – would provide a better framework than that which currently operates in England. But to be able to effectively hold to account councillors must have strengthened delay and veto powers than is currently the case in England.

When it comes to the world beyond the council the elected mayor must employ soft powers of negotiation, compromise and deal-making to bring into alignment with mayoral policy the vast array of organisations that interact within complex local policy networks. The mayor is one of many players in such networks and one of the very few that are elected or have any democratic legitimacy. But, the mayor lacks hard political powers to force change through others. Thus, we have a model of mayoral governance which does not result in any significant change to the nature of the council within which a mayor is based, where the mayor's powers are comparable to the indirectly elected leader and where the mayor and mayoral council has no enhanced power or role within local governance networks. The English elected mayor is powerful in regard to the council but in a limited sense and weak everywhere else.

Changes to the Office of Mayor
What follows is a set of suggestions for reform to the office of elected mayor that rests in traditional local government and for reforming the nature of the councils that adopt directly elected mayors. A major and necessary change to mayoral powers is that of the direct appointment and dismissal of senior council staff with such staff linked to the mayor's term of office and changing with a the election of a new mayor. The appointment of senior officers by the mayor, should however be subject to a confirmation hearing by an overview and scrutiny committee formed by the council for that task. Indeed,

appointment powers (and confirmation hearings) need to extend beyond senior officers of the council to senior officers and or chairs of public boards, agencies and bodies that operate within the boundaries of the council such as hospital trusts, fire and rescue authorities, Local Enterprise Partnerships, ports and docks, coast-guards, airports and other facilities (these appointment powers may need to be shared with other mayors, depending on the spatial scale of the organisation concerned). Alternatively elected mayors should hold the chairs of a range of public boards themselves. Linked to these extended appointment powers is the need for elected mayors to have an unlimited ability to form and appoint boards and commissions of inquiry to advise on mayoral policy, or take action delegated by the mayor, with the membership to be drawn from inside or outside the council as the mayor sees fit.

Such changes are supported by elected mayors, one of whom summed up her counter-parts' views when she stated:

> Mayors need more control over what happens outside the council; there are so many quangos, boards, trusts and they all operate in my area but I have no say over who's on them, who chairs them or what they do – mayors appointing the chairs and members would get rid of the democratic deficit.

Where more than one mayor exists in a region or area covered by some public authority or board, then the post should rotate between the elected mayors in that area; or, the mayors act as a joint appointment dismissal committee. The principle should be established that where elected mayors exist they should be automatically responsible for either holding (or appointing and dismissing), any new (and existing) sub-national public office created by government and that those appointments and dismissal powers extend to senior officers and to the chairperson of any board or authority.

Alternatively, in areas where there is an elected mayor, each public body – NHS, Police, fire and rescue, transport authority, for example – must form a geographical unit to be co-terminus with the mayoral council. Senior officers are then appointed, by the mayor, to cover that new co-terminus unit. The principles to be established here are that to ensure co-operative working between different public sector bodies and to overcome any fragmentation of provision of services and of policy and decision-making, elected mayors hold appointment and dismissal powers and public bodies must be geographically co-terminus with mayoral councils.

Continuing the theme of appointment powers, there is no real need, in practical politics, for mayoral cabinets to be limited to 10 members or limited to councillors only being apportioned to them. Indeed, such limitations on the size and membership of mayoral cabinets place a restriction on mayors' ability to select from the widest possible source of talent and expertise available and so, similarly to the power of the Mayor of London, the council mayoral cabinet should comprise of members appointed by the mayor from either outside (non-councillors) or inside the council". A mayor commented in interview:

> It makes no sense that the mayor of London can appoint a cabinet from anywhere and I have to appoint councillors. As an independent with a Labour majority that really doesn't help matters much.

A further enhancement of mayoral power is for all government departments to have a duty to consult with elected mayors on any new policy initiatives that are being developed which are appropriate to local government and public services generally. Mayors should be engaged at early stages in consultation on the development of government policy and legislation that relates to, or impacts on, local government, from whatever department it originates. Mayoral councils should be granted a legal right to challenge, through a specially designed public process, any aspects of any legislation that relate to the powers, duties, responsibilities, tasks and functions of local government. Such challenge may result in mayoral exemption, or opt-out, from policy change and legislation that lays down requirements on, or makes changes to, non-mayoral councils. What is suggested here is that the strong and accountable leadership of a mayoral council places it on a different constitutional footing to other councils – one where it is seen as an equal partner, rather than subservient agency, in the government of the country. But, such an objective will not be achieved without a fundamental reform to the nature of the councils which adopt an elected mayor.

Changes to Mayoral Councils

Again, the challenge for reformers in Ireland is to think radically about how councils with elected mayors may change and be strengthened as a governing entity. To ensure that elected mayors are able to effect political action and political change across the landscape of public services the key areas of health, policing, community safety, economic development and transport and regeneration need to rest with the elected mayor and mayoral councils irrespective of the type of council. What is required is for mayors and their council to be powerful governing bodies, rather than being seen as simply a particular type of council with the traditional series of responsibilities. The distinguishing factor must be that they are mayoral councils, not districts, counties or borough councils.

Where a council area introduces a directly elected mayor the political, financial and constitutional relationship with the centre must be re-configured to ensure effective local political leadership. To change the relationship between a mayoral council and the government requires government to alter the constitutional powers it has over local government – or at least mayoral councils. Government must cede the power to re-organise boundaries, for example, to mayoral councils and to local citizens and any proposals to merge or create larger councils must be subject to a binding local referendum in the area concerned.

One of the weaknesses in the current government's devolution agenda – with its associated combined authority elected mayors – is the absence of fiscal autonomy for those new creations. Devolution to elected mayors in traditional councils, to support mayoral political action must come with enhanced fiscal autonomy therefore central government must relinquish its powers to cap or limit, mayoral councils' taxation powers and new taxation powers need to be available to elected mayors to provide financial security and freedom, to include the following as examples, should mayors decide to take them on: Local Income Tax; local corporation tax, sales tax, tourist tax (hotel, airport, etc), car tax, local inheritance tax (Each of these taxation powers and others exist for local government across Europe and beyond). By strengthening the taxation raising powers of mayoral councils to generate income in their localities, a radically reformed financing system is created with a local bias and moreover, mayoral councils will have a far wider range of tax-raising (and spending) powers than non-mayoral councils. The new taxation powers must not be limited or altered by central government rather they should be subject to approval by local referendums. Fiscal devolution is an area where mayors and councillors do see eye to eye. A district councillor summed up the views of councillors on the matter, thus:

> We simply need the power to raise more of our own money and to be able to spend it – it's that simple. But the government – and civil servants particularly – just don't want local government to be financially independent, they lose control.

An elected mayor agreed and also summed up the view of the mayors interviewed in the research:

> Without financial autonomy, or even a severe loosening of the financial ties to the government and regulations, you won't have local government, you have local administration. I travel and visit mayors in Europe and am astounded by the taxation powers alone they have and the different sources of funds they have available. It's certainly not just about taxation but freedom to generate and spend locally.

These few changes, suggested above, in the internal and external powers of elected mayors and mayoral councils would create a powerful and distinctive model of English local government. It would require a new constitutional settlement between the centre and the mayoral localities and it rests on a notion that mayoral local government is just that: a government, with political powers extending beyond responsibilities for the provision of services. Mayoral councils need to become centres of local self-government, which have political, financial and organisational independence. Without such fundamental constitutional change elected mayors will remain politically weak and offer little else than a new way to the top political post on the council.

Conclusion
The chapter focused on the office of elected mayor as it exists in traditional English local government, rather than exploring the six new combined authority mayors elected in 2017. It did this because the new

territorial arrangements of the combined authorities do not cover the entire country, are new territorial configurations and are part of a government inspired devolution process. Moreover, elected mayors have existed in England since the first elections in 2002 and the experience so far indicates that it is an office already in need of radical reform. The need for reform is a surprise given the long journey to the introduction of elected mayors with past official inquiries into local government either shying away from recommending elected mayors (HMSO, 1967) or rejecting the notion altogether (HMSO, 1986). Government by the mid-1990s however, began to see some merit in elected mayors. Criticism of the opaque nature of local leadership and local decision-making, the lack of visibility or transparency in local government generally, became articles of faith for the centre requiring a radical solution. Elected mayors were seen as a solution, but not one which the centre placed enough faith in to introduce across the whole of English local government. Rather, as a result of the Local Government Act, 2000 local citizens could call binding referendum on introducing an elected mayor and after the Local Government and Public Involvement in Health Act, 2007 a vote of the full council became sufficient to move to an elected mayor without the need for approval in a referendum. So far however, only 16 councils (excluding the mayoralty of London) have introduced elected mayors.

Central government, which does not lack the courage to enforce change in almost any aspect of local government has been uncharacteristically restrained in the way in which elected mayors have been introduced. What has dented government enthusiasm for the wholesale introduction of elected mayors, across local government, has been the opposition from councillors, who by and large are opposed to the model, preferring the traditional council leader system, where power of appointment rests with councillors and not the public (Stoker et al., 2003; Rao, 2005; Copus, 2006). Councillors are resistant to a transfer of power from themselves to the voters when it comes to choosing the local political leader and are concerned that the direct election of the mayor might result in a candidate winning that does not come from the ruling group on the council.

The major weakness with the approach taken to elected mayors in England, and from which reformers in Ireland can draw lessons, has been reluctance, on the part of the government, to grant the office sufficient powers to be able to govern and shape the activities and outcomes of complex local policy networks. Indeed, there is also reluctance to fundamentally alter the relationship between central government and mayoral local government – seeing mayoral authorities as no different to any council in terms of powers, responsibilities and autonomy. While the centre seeks transparency, visible and accountable local leadership, it does not want those local leaders to have the powers to take a different policy direction to that of the centre, or want mayoral councils to be any harder to control than the rest of local government.

Unless the centre overcomes its reluctance to reform the existing approach to elected mayors and the powers they have an opportunity will be lost to pursue a radical devolution policy and to empower local government and local leadership. Irish reformers will need to win support at the centre and construct a cross-party coalition of support for strengthening local government at the same time as introducing elected mayors.

At the moment, in England (or at least for the British centre), centralism still trumps localism when it comes to local government and there is little sign that current devolution policies will see elected mayors in traditional English councils receive much attention but rather have to watch their new combined authority counterparts receive new powers and budgets. The danger is that these new combined authority mayors will now start to look down at what powers can be drawn upwards from local government, rather than the central government looking to council elected mayors as a recipient of the next wave of devolution – when and if it comes.

CHAPTER 6
MAYORAL GOVERNANCE: A VIEW FROM THE NORTH

Colin Knox

Background

Local government in Northern Ireland is the product of the Local Government (Ireland) Act, 1898 which established a two-tier system of councils. County boroughs (the six largest towns: Dublin, Cork, Limerick, Waterford, Belfast, Londonderry) and county councils formed the upper tier, and urban and rural districts the lower tier. Overall, this legislation established the local government structure obtaining in Ireland at the time of the establishment of the Irish Free State and devolved government of Northern Ireland. When the 'free state' was created in 1920, Northern Ireland's devolved government consisted of six counties, which formed the administrative state. Within the six counties the local government framework comprised 2 county boroughs, 6 county councils, 10 boroughs, 24 urban districts and 31 rural districts; a total of 73 local authorities, serving a population (by 1966) of about 1.4 million people. This ranged from Tandragee Urban District Council, with 1,300 inhabitants, to the city of Belfast with 407,000 (Birrell and Murie, 1980). The large number of small councils would, over time, cause significant problems in their administrative and financial capacity to deliver a range of services demanded of local government (Hayes, 1967).

The post-1920 period witnessed several controversial changes wherein "the invincibility of the Unionist local government system was carefully constructed and maintained" (O'Dowd, Rolston and Tomlinson, 1980: 98). The first step in this process began with the Local Government (Northern Ireland) Act, 1922 which: replaced proportional representation (PR) with simple majority elections; enabled the redrawing of electoral divisions and ward boundaries once PR had been removed; and, altered the franchise by incorporating property ownership as a qualification for the vote. In short, the mechanisms for Unionist hegemony were established.

Pressure for reform eventually surfaced in the 1960s from two complementary sources. First, the Northern Ireland government at Stormont started campaigning to modernise the system from March 1966 and remedy its defects – mainly the multiplicity of small local

77

authorities existing with low rateable bases and hence limited financial resources. Second, there was on-going dissatisfaction with gerrymandered electoral wards and the restricted franchise, which contributed to the disturbances ('troubles') of 1968. Local politics were dominated by sectarian considerations. Unionists controlled a disproportionate share of local authorities with disproportionately large majorities – few councils changed hands at local elections.

The Macrory Report (1970) set up to review local government divided services into regional (requiring large administrative units) and district (suitable for small areas) services. The Stormont parliament was to take responsibility for regional services and district councils would administer district services. Macrory recommended establishing 26 borough or district councils. Macrory's proposals were however overtaken by Stormont's abolition in 1972, the imposition of 'direct rule' from Westminster, and new legislation on local government (Alexander, 1982).

The most significant changes introduced by the Local Government (Northern Ireland) Act, 1972 were new local government boundaries, universal adult suffrage, and the replacement of simple plurality voting by proportional representation (the single-transferable-vote). The new district councils came into operation on 1st October 1973 and remained largely unchanged until the new devolved government in Northern Ireland launched a major review of public administration in 2002.

In spite of the councils' radically reduced powers since 1973, local government witnessed revitalised electoral competition. In 1973 there were 1,222 candidates for 526 seats compared to the previous local government election (1967) where a majority of seats were uncontested. The political composition of councils also reflected the PR electoral system where few had one party as an overall majority and greater representation of minority parties. Despite its innocuous powers, local government became immersed in wider constitutional controversy when in the 1985 elections 59 Sinn Féin councillors, representing the political wing of the Provisional Irish Republican Army (IRA), secured seats. Unionists perceived Sinn Féin's electoral strategy (the infamous mantra of the 'ballot box and armalite') as a threatening new dimension in local government and marked their displeasure by disrupting its operation. Some councils adjourned business and all 18 Unionist controlled local authorities refused to carry out normal duties. Varying degrees of conflict ensued, with occasional fistfights in council chambers over the presence of Sinn Féin (Connolly and Knox, 1988). The disruption campaign was superseded by a hard-line campaign against the Anglo-Irish Agreement of November 1985. All Unionist councils adjourned in protest, refusing to levy district rates. The courts ordered several indicted councils to resume normal business and set a rate (Knox: 1998 and 2010).

The local government elections of 1989 marked a turning point in council chambers, with a degree of moderation not unrelated to the decline in representation from the political extremes. From this stable political context an experiment in 'responsibility sharing' developed - this term evolved in deference to unionist sensitivities over the words 'power sharing'. Dungannon District Council is credited with leading the way in rotating the council chair between two main political parties, the Social Democratic and Labour Party (SDLP) and the Ulster Unionist Party (UUP), although some councils (Down, Omagh, Newry and Mourne, for example) claim to have been doing this for years in a less high-profile manner. In addition, the Enniskillen bombing of November 1987 appears to have had a profound impact on local politicians. One observer noted that councillors "felt the need to bring an end to sterile adversarial politics... and found in their opposition to political violence more in common than they had previously recognised" (Beirne, 1993: 7). Other councils followed suit in the wake of the 1989 local elections. Eleven local authorities appointed chairs/mayors and deputies from both political traditions. The power-sharing trend continued following the 1993 local elections, with 12 (of 26) councils participating. This change in local politics was to become an important portent for power sharing at the regional level in Northern Ireland (devolved government at Stormont) and eventually be significant in considering the potential for directly elected mayors.

The Review of Public Administration

Power was devolved to the Northern Ireland Assembly and its Executive Committee of Ministers on 2nd December 1999 following the signing of the Belfast (Good Friday) Agreement on 10th April 1998. The Blair Labour government saw devolution as a way of advancing the peace process by encouraging republicans and loyalists into an elected assembly and weaning them away from violence. The (then) UUP leader agreed to share power with Sinn Féin on the condition that they decommissioned their weaponry. They didn't, and the Assembly was suspended on 11th February 2000. One of the first significant administrative reforms the devolved government proposed was a *Review of Public Administration* which it launched in 2002. Its remit was to review the existing arrangements for the accountability, administration and delivery of public services in Northern Ireland, and to bring forward options for reform which were consistent with the arrangements and principles of the Belfast Agreement (Knox and Carmichael, 2006).

The Review of Public Administration was however overtaken by the fitful process of devolution which continued until the (then) British Secretary of State for Northern Ireland (John Reid) reinstated direct rule from Westminster in October 2002 due to "a lack of trust and loss of confidence on both sides of the community" (Knox and Carmichael, 2010: 83). Direct Rule remained in place until after the St Andrews Agreement and its legal outworking in the Northern Ireland (St Andrews Agreement) Act, 2006 which came into force with the restoration of devolved government. Elections took place in March 2007 and devolution to a power-sharing Assembly was restored on 8th May 2007, operated for almost ten years, and collapsed in January 2017. New elections took place in March 2017 over a financial scandal (Renewable Heat Incentive Scheme) involving the Democratic Unionist Party (DUP).

The upshot of political turmoil at the regional level meant that the final outcomes of the Review of Public Administration for local government in Northern Ireland were not implemented until 1st April 2015. Although the original claim of the Review was to create strong local government, the final product was little more than the addition of a small number of relatively minor functions to existing services and the reduction from 26 councils to 11 new local authorities as set out in table 6.1.

Table 6.1: Northern Ireland Councils	
Responsible for	Not responsible for
Waste collection and disposal	Education
Local development planning	Health and personal social services
Building control	Roads
Environmental protection and improvement	Fire
Leisure services and local tourism	Police
Arts, heritage and cultural facilities	Transport

Street cleaning	Public Housing
Food safety	Urban regeneration
Local economic development	Libraries
Off-street parking	Trading standards
Community planning and general power of competence	Street lighting

An overview of the 11 new councils shows that they are relatively small stakeholders in the wider public sector as follows:

- Average council population = 167,300 people;
- Largest Council (Belfast: 336,830); Smallest (Fermanagh and Omagh: 114,992);
- Total gross spending (11 councils) = £793.5m;
- Per capita spend across 11 councils = £344;
- Amount raised via district rates = £612m ;
- Northern Ireland Executive Budget = £10.3b;
- Local government accounts for 7.7% of overall public spending in Northern Ireland.

Despite the emasculated form of local government which operated in Northern Ireland from 1973 until its reform in 2015, councils have been a consistent and relatively stable form of governance. During long periods of Direct Rule from Westminster, they were the only locally accountable decision making forum. Although their early work on power-sharing was superseded by wider political developments, the legacy of these operating principles have carried over into the new councils. Table 2 shows the political composition of the Mayor/Chairs and deputy Mayor/Vice Chair of the 11 new councils at the time of writing (March 2017).

Table 6.2: Power Sharing in Councils			
	Mayor/Chair	Deputy Mayor/Vice Chair	Population
Antrim and Newtownabbey	DUP	SDLP	139,996
Ards and North Down	Alliance	DUP	157,931
Armagh, Banbridge Craigavon	Sinn Fein	DUP	205,711

Belfast	DUP	Sinn Fein	336,830
Causeway Coast and Glens	SDLP	UUP	142,303
Derry and Strabane	DUP	SDLP	149,198
Fermanagh and Omagh	SDLP	UUP	114,992
Lisburn and Castlereagh	UUP	Alliance	138,627
Mid and East Antrim	DUP	UUP	136,642
Mid Ulster	UUP	SDLP	142,895
Newry, Mourne and Down	SDLP	DUP	175,403
Total			**1,840,498**

Aside from Mid and East Antrim, all councils currently operate power sharing leadership arrangements. Does the recently reformed local government system therefore lend itself to directly elected mayors?

Directly Elected Mayors?

The English debate on locally elected mayors is difficult to 'read-across' to the context of Northern Ireland. Hambleton and Sweeting (2014), for example, in reviewing the research on the experience of Britain since the inception of directly elected mayors introduced by the Local Government Act, 2000 outline both sides of the debate. On the one hand, proponents argue that they improve the voice of local people in influencing local affairs and hence strengthen local democracy. On the other hand, critics argue that mayoral governance is elitist given the concentration of power in the hands of one person (Hambleton and Sweeting, 2014). Similarly, research by Copus (2004) which highlighted the potential for elected mayors in England to change the party political dynamic between the electorate and traditional parties, seems unlikely in the context of Northern Ireland, given voting loyalties to unionist/loyalist and nationalist/republican cleavages. As is often the case when examining the United Kingdom, Northern Ireland is different.

The key contribution, which mayors/chairs at local-government level have made in Northern Ireland, is to embed the principle of power sharing that has been pivotal to the Belfast (Good Friday) Agreement. Hence, what had been happening in local government for some time, presided over by chairs, mayors or lord mayors, became the blueprint for a devolved Northern Ireland Assembly. Legislative Assembly members (MLAs) are elected by proportional representation (STV) and the election of the chair and deputy-chair of the Assembly, main committees, and the power-sharing executive are made on the basis of proportionality using d'Hondt. Key decisions are taken on a cross-community basis (either through parallel consent or weighted majority). The potency of mayoral symbolism and how this has been used in the wider political process in Northern Ireland goes well beyond the functional importance of local government as a democratic entity (Knox, 2007). As one leader-writer put it at the beginning of the 2001 local government elections:

> Some council chambers, most notably Belfast City Hall, once earned a reputation for being sectarian bear pits. But tensions have eased and local government has played its part in changing the face of Northern Ireland politics. Although mayoral rotation has not worked everywhere, many councils blazed a trail for the peace process by demonstrating that power sharing can be a reality (McAdam, 2001: 1).

The contribution by councils to 'working' power sharing at local level has been hard fought, and not without major controversy in some authorities which cling to the vestiges of majoritarianism and unionist domination. This is particularly true where Sinn Féin is vying for the post of chair, mayor or lord mayor, the political symbolism of which is simply too much for die-hard unionists to accept. The case is best illustrated by Sinn Féin's success in securing the post of Lord Mayor of Belfast for the first time in its history in June 2002 when Alex Maskey was elected the first Sinn Féin Lord Mayor of Belfast.

Discussions about the possibility of directly elected mayors/chairs in the Northern Irish context have been mostly rejected as divisive and likely to compound sectarianism. For example, in a debate in Derry City Council on the merits of having a mayor directly elected by the public every 4 years, the (then) DUP mayor (Mildred Garfield) argued she would be the city's last unionist mayor if the proposal became a reality. Given Derry's large nationalist majority, it is highly likely that a public vote would displace existing power-sharing arrangements to rotate the mayoralty between parties with a nationalist/republican first citizen. This would do little to foster harmony and good relations in the city. This is why there is a range of statutory safeguards built into the operation of the new councils to ensure confidence and trust. The safeguards include reference to the election of the chair, mayor or lord mayor of local authorities and a more detailed explication of his/her civic leadership role.

Beyond these important political considerations, however, a number of economists [(Simpson (2015); Webb (2015); and Birnie (2016)] argue that Northern Ireland should be interested in the Northern Powerhouse example comprising the three large regions in the North of England: the North East, North West and Yorkshire, and the Humber. This was the former Conservative Chancellor's (George Osborne) idea of maximising devolution (so called 'devo-max'), which would combine local authorities, directly elect mayors, and give councils new fiscal powers. All of this was aimed at driving change at the regional level. Writing recently with former Mayor of New York (Michael Bloomberg), Osborne claimed:

> Linking together the cities and towns of the North of England, and devolving greater powers to their mayors, would allow these cities to enjoy the kind of advantages of scale that bigger cities such as London and New York enjoy, and which they have used to great effect. In other words, by joining forces the whole of a region can be bigger than its parts... to make this happen most effectively, these cities need directly elected mayors (Osborne and Bloomberg, 2017: 26).

Belfast as the Northern (Ireland) Powerhouse?
Belfast City Council is the most obvious example of the Osborne model in the Northern Ireland context where it could act as a coordinating body to drive social and economic change and, with this, follow the approach of a directly elected mayor. Sir Richard Needham, the longest serving former Direct Rule Minister in Northern Ireland, recently argued that having a directly elected mayor in Belfast would offer leadership for the whole region: "Bristol, under a directly elected mayor, is one of the ten most exciting cities in the world, whereas Belfast is way down the list because it doesn't have the leadership. That

is a real problem" (Needham, 2017: 12). The difficulty with granting Belfast 'Northern Powerhouse' status is that it would rival Stormont. This would be politically unpopular with Members of the Legislative Assembly, some of whom served their political apprenticeships in local government and see regional parliament as an upward career shift.

A test of the regional government's commitment to a stronger local government comes in the form of urban regeneration and community development, functions originally promised to transfer from central to local government following the Review of Public Administration and the formation of the new councils. These functions were seen as complementary to additional powers given to local government in 2015 for local planning, economic development and tourism, all of which would have empowered councils to lead and reshape their entire communities. However, in November 2016, the Minister for Communities announced that: "I do not intend to bring forward proposals to extend my Department's urban regeneration and community development powers to local government during this mandate" (Givan, 2016: 1).

This, despite the fact Belfast City Council is pushing under its new Chief Executive for 'city deal' status to promote the physical, economic and community development infrastructure similar to other cities in Britain. As one commentator put it: "Greater Belfast has over one third of Northern Ireland's population, well over half its economy and no regional rival as an urban centre. It could hollow Stormont out to the point of irrelevance" (Emerson, 2016: 25). The fact that local government has its own source of local tax raising powers (district rates) also adds to the argument for greater independence and more direct accountability for spending through a directly elected mayor. In 2016/17, for example, the new 11 councils in Northern Ireland will raise £612m through local district rates (Department for Communities, 2016). Stormont then levies a regional rate on top of this amount for services which are within the remit of councils in other parts of the United Kingdom, and both district and regional rates are collected through councils. This has been a long-standing grievance in local government that councillors are held electorally accountable for a proportion of spending over which they have no control. The rationale for having elected mayors was "to make it clearer to councillors and the public alike where the responsibility for a particular decision lay" (Sandford, 2016: 4). If local government in Northern Ireland were to be given statutory powers to elect mayors, then this would demand a radical rethink of the current district and regional rating system. The concern, despite the current dysfunctionality of Stormont, is that if Belfast acquired city deal status, similar to Greater Manchester, Bristol, Leeds, Liverpool, Greater Manchester etc., then the case for a devolved Assembly and nine government departments becomes difficult to justify. However, the political importance of a regional assembly and its association with the peace process makes dismantling this edifice unrealistic, certainly in the short to medium term.

There are three other key points of relevance here. First, local councils prior to the 2015 reforms operated under the shadow of Belfast City Council (by far the largest at that stage) and often felt unfairly and negatively represented as a sector by the council. Moves by Belfast City Council at this point (now more comparable in population terms) to elect a mayor would prompt a reaction from the 4 other cities in Northern Ireland (Armagh, Derry, Lisburn and Newry), the smallest of which has a population of 138,627 people (Lisburn and Castlereagh). Population scale is unlikely to warrant a city deal of the type now brokered in Britain and an associated directly elected mayor. Second, if one looks at the current political composition of Belfast City Council following the 2014 local government elections, Sinn Féin is the largest political party with 19 seats (out of 60 seats)[31]. The Alliance Party holds the overall balance of power between unionists and nationalists with 8 seats. A contest for a directly elected mayor would heighten sectarian voting and place Alliance Party supporters in an invidious position. The third important point is that the political landscape has changed in Britain and the new British Prime Minister (Theresa May) has jettisoned Osborne's pledges to require city regions to have directly elected mayors in order to receive devolution deals from central government. Reflecting on the experience of Britain's 16 current elected mayors, Copus (2016) concludes that they have not become key national political players or established international profiles which more generally reflects "the lack of genuine local self-government existing in England and centralist attitudes".

---

[31] Belfast City Council composition: Sinn Féin 19; Democratic Unionist Party 13; Alliance 8; Social Democratic and Labour Party 7; Ulster Unionist Party 7; Progressive Unionist Party 3; Traditional Unionist Voice 1; Green Party 1; People before Profit 1.

The experience of devolution in Northern Ireland to date would suggest the same centripetal tendencies. Stormont has so far proved unwilling, despite the rhetoric of support for strong local government, to devolve powers and functions to local councils. Without these, the role of a directly elected mayor presiding over minor powers would be vacuous and merely compound sectarianism as the electorate resort to type and vote 'for their own'. The debate on having a directly elected mayor in Dublin is also premised on four pre-existing councils working for the region with significant powers in transportation, housing, energy, traffic, planning and so on. The prospect of this happening was deemed unlikely according to Hayes, the Fine Gael MEP for Dublin:

> The mayor must have power to make decisions for Dublin as a region. This would mean central government transferring powers...but don't under estimate the centralising tendency within the upper ranks of our public administration. We have a poor record of sharing and devolving power. It's not in the political and public sector DNA (Hayes, 2016: 19).

This point could easily be made about the Stormont government in Northern Ireland.

Conclusions

The lessons from Britain, and the prospective concerns in Dublin, clearly resonant in any possible discussion about having an elected mayor in Belfast. To be successful, mayoral governance in Belfast would require a city with significantly more powers than it currently has. It would also require voters to look beyond traditional unionist/nationalist cleavages in the wider interests of city-wide prosperity, and magnanimity from Stormont that Belfast City Council was not competing for regional significance which could threaten its raison d'être. On these grounds alone, the prospect of having a directly elected mayor in Belfast sometime soon looks highly unlikely. Moreover, the political symbolism associated with power sharing in local government militates against vesting power in the hands of an individual as a directly elected mayor. The peace process is predicated on a devolved power-sharing regional assembly in Northern Ireland. Despite the problems associated with Stormont as an elected forum, stronger local government of a scale consistent with other British or Irish cities which have or will have elected mayors is unrealistic in Northern Ireland. An elected mayor would compound sectarianism by vesting power in the hands of the majority community, which will differ across councils, but nonetheless resurrect fears of hegemony and abuse of privilege once directly associated with local government from the period 1922-1973. There is no appetite for this return to majoritarianism which would be the inevitable result of introducing directly elected mayors in Northern Ireland. The economics for having a directly elected Mayor in Belfast City Council are overshadowed by political apprehension of reverting to the 'bad old days'

CHAPTER 7
MAYORAL OPTIONS FOR DUBLIN: SPATIAL AND POLITICAL CONSIDERATIONS

Mark Callanan

Introduction

The aim of this chapter is to present some of the choices facing Irish policy-makers over executive arrangements in local government. Ireland has had an 'on-off' debate over whether or not to establish a directly elected mayor (either for all city and county councils or for the Dublin area) for the last two decades and more. And it seems as though this debate is something that is unlikely to 'go away', given the issue features regularly in the manifestos of various political parties.

There are in fact multiple options available for such an office, in terms of both the powers of a mayor and the spatial scale of the mandate of a mayor, based on internal experience. Aside from mayoral systems, there are also other options for increasing the executive role of elected members, such as cabinet-based models. In addition, of course, there is always the standard 'do nothing' option – that is the option of retaining the existing system of council and manager (recently retitled chief executive). There would also appear to be several political considerations (and obstacles) that seem to confront the prospective establishment of a directly elected mayor for Dublin and indeed other city-regions/local authority areas.

The chapter sets the context by firstly outlining a short overview of the debate over mayoral models to date in Ireland, identifying key milestones and features of the debate. Second, it highlights a number of executive options for local government drawing on international research, suggesting that mayoral models are not the only option that might be considered in this respect. Third, the question of the geographical mandate of a 'Dublin' mayor is addressed, presenting a series of options. Fourth, some options around the specific powers of a mayor are identified. Finally, the chapter concludes by considering some of the political (and possibly public) obstacles to establishing a directly elected mayor.

Debate over Directly Elected Mayors in Ireland – A Short History

It is not the intention of this chapter to delve into the long lineage of the office of mayor in Irish history (see for example MacCarthaigh and Callanan, 2007). Rather the emphasis here is on the debates over whether or not to establish an office of directly elected mayor to serve in office for the full five-year term of the council, as opposed to the existing system whereby mayors are selected by the council to serve in office for one year. Some of the reasons why such proposals have not been implemented to date are considered in the final section.

In terms of relatively recent discussions over a directly elected mayor for Dublin, we may take our starting point as the reorganisation of local government in Dublin in the early 1990s. In conjunction with the division of the old Dublin County Council into three new county council areas, proposals were aired by some political parties suggesting the need to establish a directly elected mayor who would hold office for four years to give a Dublin-wide perspective (Zimmerman, 1994). These proposals were not followed up.

The original provisions of the Local Government Act, 2001 (Part 5) had provided that from 2004, the chairpersons of all county and city councils would be directly elected by the local population of the area, and would hold office for a five-year term. The elections for mayor were to take place on the same day as elections for local councils, and term-limits were set out in the legislation: mayors were to be ineligible to hold office for more than two consecutive terms (i.e. 10 years in total). As we know, these provisions for directly elected mayors, while passed into law in 2001, never came of anything. Subsequent legislation was passed in 2003 that effectively repealed the provisions in advance of their implementation in 2004.

The 2001 Act did not provide for any additional executive powers for this proposed new mayoral position, despite the proposal that office-holders would be directly elected and would serve a much longer term. However, one could envisage how such a position might eventually have been allocated additional responsibilities and powers over time. Equally, the Minister for Environment and Local Government behind the initiative at that time, Noel Dempsey TD, argued that the enhanced mandate would in itself make the position stronger. Speaking in the Dáil, he argued that direct election would increase the accountability and visibility of the position, and that such a mayor would be able to draw on "powerful democratic legitimacy to speak and negotiate on behalf of the whole community with influence well beyond any formal powers and with the capacity to bring together the various elements of local governance. Experience elsewhere bears this out if the opportunities being presented are grasped and acted upon in a spirit of collaboration for the common good" (Dáil debates, 8th March 2001, Vol. 532: col. 833).

It was also argued that the position would provide a personification for county and city councils, and give the local authority a more visible presence in the local area, given that the mayor would serve a longer term. Given the general media interest in personalities, it was suggested that directly elected mayors might generate greater interest in local politics, the implicit suggestion being that because the position changes every year, the current office of mayor is not a particularly visible position amongst the public at large and many citizens are unaware of the identity of their local mayor.

While the Local Government Act, 2001 had initially foreseen directly elected mayors in each county and city council area, the 2008 Green Paper on Local Government proposed a directly elected mayor elected by residents of the four Dublin local authorities (i.e. a single mayor covering both Dublin City and County, elected by voters in the Dublin City, Dún Laoghaire-Rathdown, Fingal and South Dublin local authorities). Under this proposal, the four local authorities would continue to provide local government services, but the mayor would have regional strategic planning responsibilities for the Dublin area in issues such as spatial planning, public transport, housing, waste management and water services.

In principle, the Green Paper also supported the idea of directly elected mayors in each city and county council area. While the office would largely build on the existing delineation of responsibility between reserved and executive functions, one suggestion was that a directly elected mayor could take on some policy initiation responsibilities, for example through the directly elected mayor being responsible for presenting the draft annual budget or the draft development plan for decision by the elected council. Another option raised in the Green Paper was to extend the position of directly elected mayors to other 'city regions', and particularly gateway cities and hubs identified under the National Spatial Strategy (Government of Ireland, 2008).

On foot of the Green Paper, the government published a Bill (the Local Government (Mayor and Regional Authority of Dublin) Bill 2010) proposing to establish a directly elected mayor for Dublin (to be elected by residents of the four Dublin local authorities). Under the proposed legislation, the Dublin mayor would have had a role in establishing the policy framework for land-use planning, housing, transport and traffic management, waste management and water services for the Dublin area, with the four Dublin local authorities retaining operational responsibility for service provision in these areas. However, the bill fell with the dissolution of the Dáil in 2011.

The 2012 Putting People First reform programme also stated that while a directly elected mayor for the Dublin region would in principle entail a number of benefits, the text of the document expended some time making the case against such a move, for example pointing to a number of requirements or preconditions for establishing such an office. It suggested that such an office would need substantial functions and budgeting powers, which would have to be transferred from either central but particularly from local government. It also stressed the need to ensure the mayor's powers do not duplicate those of local authorities, the potential for such an office to diminish the role of elected local councillors, and commenting that the "success or otherwise of such an office is likely to depend to a significant extent on the calibre of the incumbent" (Government of Ireland, 2012: 139) – although one could arguably also make this observation about central government Ministers!

The Putting People First programme proposed that a forum or colloquium of local councillors from the four Dublin local authorities be convened to analyse the different options for the powers and role of a directly elected mayor, and that any subsequent proposal to emerge would be put to a plebiscite of those eligible to vote in local elections in the four Dublin local authorities.

These proposals were in turn reflected in Part 11 of the Local Government Reform Act, 2014, which essentially put in place a three-step process whereby an office of directly elected mayor could be established:

- Initiation of proposals and approval by each of the four Dublin local authorities – Following proposals for a mayoral position published by a forum representing each of the four local authorities, each of the four local authorities would have to approve these proposals by resolution;

- Public ballot – A plebiscite would have been held on the same day of the 2014 local elections, whereby voters in the four Dublin local authorities would have been asked to approve or reject the proposal to establish a directly elected mayor;
- Ministerial proposals to the Oireachtas – If a majority of voters approved of the proposal to establish a directly elected mayor, the issue would then revert to the Minister who would, within 2 years, have had to present proposals to the Oireachtas for establishing a directly elected mayor for Dublin, or "a statement of his or her reasons for not making proposals for legislation" (section 69).

In the event, the proposals never proceeded beyond the first step. The colloquium of the elected members of the four Dublin local authorities unveiled draft proposals for a mayoral position in late 2013. These proposals involved establishing a Dublin mayor with executive responsibilities in housing, planning, waste management, transport, community and traffic policing, fire services, economic development and tourism, suggesting that personnel and financial resources would have to be transferred from a series of national agencies to the Dublin mayoral office. The colloquium also proposed giving the mayor a strategic role in setting policy for the Dublin area in fields such as policing, water, education and health (Kelly, 2013). However, in order for the plebiscite to proceed in conjunction with the 2014 local elections, each of the four Dublin local authorities had to approve a resolution that the proposals from the forum be voted on by plebiscite. While a majority of the councillors on Dublin City Council, and on Dún Laoghaire-Rathdown and South Dublin County Councils voting in favour of holding the plebiscite, the elected council in Fingal County Council rejected the proposal to hold a plebiscite, and the vote was not held in 2014 (Quinlivan, 2014).

More recently, the 2016 Programme for a Partnership Government contained a commitment to 'consider' the introduction of directly elected mayors in cities. In addition, the Terms of Reference for two separate Expert Advisory Group established by central government to examine local government arrangements in Cork and Galway both provided for consideration being given to whether a directly elected mayor should be established as part of any revised local government structures in these areas.

This 'on-off' debate over whether or not to establish a directly elected mayor, either in selected areas or in all local authorities, shows both the enduring attractiveness of the idea of directly elected mayors for some, but equally the resistance to such a position being established from others. In terms of the rationale for such a position, the 2008 Green Paper (Government of Ireland 2008) presented a number of reasons for directly elected mayors including:

- Directly elected mayors would enhance the democratic legitimacy of local government and the claim of the office-holder of mayor to represent the local area;
- Directly elected mayors would have greater visibility and give a higher profile to the position and to local government generally, both within the local community and through the likelihood of increased media attention given to the position;
- Directly elected mayors would provide greater continuity given that those elected would hold office for 5 years, instead of one.

One could potentially add to this list the possibility that a mayor elected across the city/county could arguably take a more city or county-wide perspective of the problems facing the area, in contrast to local councillors who might have a greater focus on the needs of their specific local electoral area within the county or city.

For those cautioning against the idea, the possibility that mayoral elections could be dominated by 'single issue' or 'personality' has been raised as one possible drawback. Sources of opposition to the idea are further discussed in the final section of the chapter below.

Different Local Government Executive Models – Mayors, Cabinets, Councils and Managers

It is worth putting the debate in Ireland over directly elected mayors in a comparative context, given that this is a discussion that has echoes in many other jurisdictions. Alongside managerial reforms and the development of new attempts to engage citizens in decision-making, a core theme of local government reform processes across Europe and beyond has been changes to political executive arrangements (see for example John, 2001; Denters and Rose, 2005; Dollery, Garcea and LeSage, 2008; Loughlin, Hendriks and Lidström, 2011). A series of comparative analyses have been published focussing on mayoral systems and political executive models (Mouritzen and Svara 2002; Berg and Rao 2002; Bäck, Heinelt, and Magnier 2006; Garrard 2007).

There exist significant differences between states (and sometimes within states) in the executive role of office-holders in local government, and the interplay between the political elected office-holders and the administrative branch within local government, and the relative balance of powers and responsibilities between different actors. Key actors in this respect can include the following:

- Mayors: The powers of mayors vary considerably, ranging from strong mayors with extensive executive decision-making powers to weaker mayors playing a largely ceremonial role. Mayors may also be directly elected by voters or indirectly elected (appointed by the local council) – these are often given different titles in different jurisdictions, including burgomaster, provost, or in the Irish case Cathaoirleach;
- Cabinets: In some countries, political executive responsibilities are not vested in a single individual (such as a strong mayor) but rather to a small group of local council members, typically with individual cabinet members taking responsibility for specific local government service areas – again different titles can be used in this respect such as municipal executive, executive committee, or cabinet;
- Council: The role of the council might be the primary political authority within local government, or in some systems the role of the council might be primarily to monitor and scrutinise the decisions of the directly elected mayor. The council typically works as a collective body but with many issues deliberated on in advance in service-specific committees of the council;
- Manager/Chief Executive: The role of chief executives as head of administration varies across jurisdiction. In some countries, the position is closely associated with elected office-holders, either through the local council or through a strong mayor, while in others the chief executive has considerable discretion, managerial autonomy and delegated responsibilities in terms of

implementing policy frameworks – titles used can range from chief executive, city manager or county manager, or secretary-general.

Based on the role of these different actors, Mouritzen and Svara (2002) distinguish between four different executive models used in local government, namely: the strong mayor model; the committee-leader model; the collective model; and the council-manager model (they place Ireland in the category of the council-manager model). While different countries might illustrate specific variants of each of the models, they represent 'ideal-types' and ways of distinguishing between different executive forms within local government.

The strong mayor model entails placing most executive powers in the office of mayor, who might be directly or indirectly elected. Generally collegiate bodies such as the elected council or council committees will be subservient to the mayor under this model. Often the chief executive serves at the discretion of the mayor, with the mayor responsible for day-to-day administration, and in larger local authorities the mayor may appoint senior staff. This approach has a long tradition in North America, although statistically only a minority of American local authorities use the strong mayor model – however the strong mayor model is prominent in the US because it tends to be the model used in the very large cities.

Mouritzen and Svara (2002) suggest that local government in France, Spain, Portugal and Italy falls under this model. The strong mayor model has also become increasingly popular in other parts of the world, including South America and other parts of Europe. For example, Germany, Austria, Italy, Poland and Hungary moved to establish directly elected mayors during the 1990s. While countries such as France and Spain might formally have indirectly elected (i.e. council-appointed) mayors, given that these states use party list electoral systems, local elections can also arguably be said to be de facto direct elections for mayors. This is because voters know that the candidate at the top of each party list is that party's candidate for mayor, and that by voting for a certain party list they are also implicitly supporting that party's lead candidate as mayor (Kuhlmann and Wollmann, 2014).

However the move towards directly elected mayors is by no means universal. Despite the attention given to US mayors (particularly in larger cities), most US municipalities use the council-manager system with an elected council and a city manager appointed to manage local government services (see below).

The committee-leader model involves an individual that is clearly identified as a political figurehead (who may be called mayor but may also be referred to by other titles, such as 'council leader' in the English local government system), but where this individual shares executive powers with other collegiate bodies, including the elected council and committees of the council, and with the chief executive. Mouritzen and Svara (2002) suggest that local government in Denmark, Sweden, and Britain fall under this model, although from the 2000s most local authorities in England established a cabinet structure more akin to the collective model (see below).

The collective model involves most executive power being placed in a collective group, executive board or cabinet-style structure. Members of the cabinet are nominated by the council, and chaired by a mayor. However executive powers rest with the cabinet as a collective, rather than with the mayor. In some jurisdictions the members of the cabinet/executive are referred to as aldermen. Members of the cabinet might have particular responsibilities for particular service areas or departments of the local authority. While members of the cabinet must be elected to the local council in some places, in others the council may choose 'outsiders' to serve in the cabinet. In many ways therefore, this model resonates with the approach used at national level in parliamentary systems like Ireland, whereby the electorate choose national parliamentarians to serve in Dáil Éireann, who themselves select a subset of their members to serve in an executive capacity as Ministers in government. Mouritzen and Svara (2002) suggest that local government in the Netherlands and Belgium are examples of this collective model, to which we might also add most local authorities in England.

Under the council-manager model, executive powers and managerial autonomy is delegated to a professional manager to run services within a policy and budgetary framework adopted by the council. The manager is responsible for staffing issues, and may make proposals for policy and budgetary decisions for approval by the council. In the council-manager model, the manager is responsible to the elected council as a collective, rather than being individually responsible to a mayor (as can be the case for chief executives in other models). While in some places using this model the mayor might be directly elected, in others the mayor elected by the council, and either way the role of mayor tends to be limited to chairing and ceremonial responsibilities. In most countries using the council-manager model, the council also appoints and can dismiss the manager.

Along with Ireland, Mouritzen and Svara (2002) suggest that most US cities, as well as local government in Finland, Australia, and to some extent Norway are examples of the 'council-manager' form. Howard and Sweeting (2007) add New Zealand to this list of countries using variants of the 'council-manager' model. This reflects the significant role played by professional managers and chief executives in these systems, but also in other countries too (Klausen and Magnier, 1998). While much prominence is given to the mayoral model in the United States (where it is the dominant executive form in the very large and therefore the most prominent cities), statistics suggest that more and more US cities are adopting the council-manager model. The proportion of US local authorities using the council-manager system went from a third in 1990 to a half in 2005, while there was a similar decline in the use of the mayoral model during the same period (Svara and Hoene, 2008). The council-manager system remains the model used in over half of US local authorities (International City/County Management Association 2014).

Indeed, before rushing headlong towards the model of directly elected mayor, it is worth giving careful consideration to the merits of retaining the council-manager model as an option. A review of 76 studies comparing the performance of US local authorities using the 'council-manager' form and US local authorities using stronger mayoral models found that some studies suggest that the council-manager form is characterised by less conflict between local council members, greater levels of management innovation, and is associated with better quality services and greater levels of effectiveness, albeit with data suggesting that the council-manager system is also associated with lower turnouts at local elections (Carr, 2015).

Options for Spatial Scale

One question that arises over the potential establishment of a directly elected mayor for Dublin is what the geographical mandate of a Dublin mayor should be? In essence, what constitutes Dublin? The most recent proposals have tended to reflect a view that the mandate of the mayor would concern what might be popularly called the 'GAA Dublin', namely the four Dublin local authorities constituting the Dublin City Council area, plus the Dún Laoghaire-Rathdown, Fingal and South Dublin County Council areas. However, other possible geographical areas have also been suggested as part of the ongoing debate over the office.

A number of options are identified below, in ascending order of scale.

As a first option, the position of directly elected mayor might exist for the Dublin City Council area only – in essence this was what was envisaged in the 2001 Act, albeit with elected mayors also serving the other three Dublin local authorities as well. When Fingal County Council rejected the proposals for a plebiscite on a directly elected mayor for the four Dublin local authority areas in 2014, it also observed that proposals could be advanced for a directly elected mayor for the Dublin city area. According to Census 2016, the population of the area of Dublin city in 2016 was over 554,000 persons.

A second option might be that a single mayor might serve the four Dublin local authority areas – this was the option provided for under the 2014 Act, while the 2008 Green Paper also suggested that "this configuration would have the greatest legitimacy in terms of traditional allegiance" (Government of Ireland, 2008: 42). This was also the area provided for under the 2010 Bill. This area had a combined population of 1.35 million in 2016.

A third option might be to ignore local authority and administrative boundaries, and define a Dublin metropolitan area based on spatial planning criteria, such as a threshold proportion of people living in an area that commute into Dublin city on a regular basis – this might mean the area concerned would extend to large parts of southern and eastern Meath, north Kildare and north Wicklow. While involving the delineation of a new boundary, such an approach might be merited particularly if the powers of the mayor were to be focused on areas such as transport or land use planning.

A fourth (perhaps administratively neater) delineation would be that the mayor would serve what has frequently been termed the Greater Dublin Area, namely the four Dublin local authorities, plus all of Meath, Kildare and Wicklow. This area had a combined population of 1.9 million in 2016.

A fifth option would be to make the mayor's mandate align with the newly configured Eastern and Midland Regional Assembly area, by which the mayor's mandate would extend to the four Dublin local authorities, plus Louth, Meath, Laois, Offaly, Longford, Westmeath, Kildare and Wicklow. This area had a combined population of 2.33 million in 2016.

Current Mayoral Powers

While the current position of mayor is seen as a largely ceremonial position, it is worth noting that the mayor under Irish law does have a limited number of powers (MacCarthaigh and Callanan, 2007):

- The mayor may request information from the chief executive related to any local authority activity;
- The mayor may call a special meeting of the council, either on his / her own initiative or on foot of a request by five or more council members;
- If the local authority administration has to incur additional expenditure in emergency cases (for example to minimise a threat to public health or safety or to the environment) beyond that authorised by the local council in its annual budget, the mayor must be informed and given details 'without delay', and the members of the council must be informed at the next practicable meeting;
- The provisions on declarations of interest, and ethics and standards in public office, provide that where a possible contravention of these rules concerns a local authority employee, this is brought to the attention of the chief executive. However, in the case of a possible contravention by an elected member or the chief executive himself or herself, the matter is referred to the mayor, who may initiate an investigation, disciplinary procedures, or refer the matter to the Director of Public Prosecutions.

In Dublin, some Lord Mayors have availed of the option of establishing a Commission to discuss and address an issue of particular concern (examples have included crime and community policing, local government financing, and housing). This work is legitimised by the ceremonial status of the Lord Mayor as the civic leader of the city. The perceived success of these initiatives depends on whether the issue in question can grab the public eye. Dublin City has also instituted a Lord Mayor's Award, which recognises the work of those making a special contribution to those working in the community. However, it remains the case that the influence of mayors is considered to relate more to the ability of the incumbent to pursue their agenda rather than any formal powers (MacCarthaigh and Callanan, 2007).

Options for Mayoral Powers
There is no shortage of examples from other jurisdictions over the possible powers of a directly elected mayor might have – these are touched on above and are addressed by other contributors. Broadly speaking however, one could envisage the mayor having a mix of strategic and executive powers.

In some areas, the mayor might play a primarily strategic or coordination role. The role of the mayor might, for some issues, be focused on the adoption of regional strategies or frameworks, but service provision left to local authorities or national agencies to deliver services within these frameworks. Thus the mayor might have a role in adopting regional strategies in areas such as land use planning, public transport, housing, policing, economic development, water provision, waste management, and so forth. Local authorities, public utilities, enterprise agencies and other bodies would then have to ensure their services aligned with the regional strategies. This approach was the one favoured by the 2008 Green Paper and subsequent 2010 Bill – although the emphasis was placed on giving the mayor a strategic remit over areas that are already the responsibility of local government, rather than over areas currently managed by national agencies.

Some options for executive powers might include some power of initiation within local government. For example, the mayor could be given a formal role in the preparation of draft budgets or development plans, presenting these to the local council for councillors to decide on. These had been proposed as options in the 2008 Green Paper.

Another more radical option would be to transfer whole areas of executive responsibility to the mayor, for example in areas such as public transport, economic development, waste management, infrastructure provision – such an option would involve the potential transfer of responsibilities (and accompanying personnel and financial resources) from local authorities and a variety of national agencies and bodies. This was the approach advocated by the 2013 proposals made by the colloquium of Dublin local authorities.

The experience with devolution in Ireland has not been a promising one. We have only limited examples of functions exercised by national agencies or central government departments being delegated to local government. Thus a reasonable prediction might be that should a mayoral office be established, most or even all of the powers of the mayor could constitute responsibilities currently exercised by local authorities, rather than responsibilities currently exercised by central government or national agencies. Both the provisions of the 2010 Bill and the wording of the 2012 Putting People First programme also suggest that, should a mayoral office for Dublin be established, its role is more likely to entail transfer of powers from local government rather than national agencies.

Political Considerations

Creating an office of directly elected mayor in Dublin raises significant political questions. The most recent proposals would have involved establishing a mayor for the four Dublin local authority areas, an area with a combined population of 1.35 million people. Should such an office be established, a candidate entering office would arguably have a stronger electoral mandate than any national politician, with the exception of the President.

While directly elected mayors have their supporters in the political system, they have also aroused largely muted opposition from many national and local politicians. While proposals for directly elected mayors might feature in party manifestos, it is clear that many political parties are far from united on this issue (MacCarthaigh and Callanan, 2007). The 2008 Green Paper (Government of Ireland, 2008) noted that the provisions in the 2001 Act on directly elected mayors were opposed by a majority of councillors (see also Kenny, 2003). However, they were also opposed by the bulk of TDs and Senators.

One might conclude that thus far, proposals for directly elected mayors have simply come up against too many interests who might be likely to lose out were such a position created (some of these were identified in the 2008 Green Paper (Government of Ireland, 2008)). While the idea retains some popularity and has regularly featured in party political manifestos in different elections, it also clearly faces quiet opposition from some actors.

Firstly, opposition might come from cabinet, and more broadly from some within central government, who might reasonably expect directly elected mayors to lead to a more vocal local government sector that is more independent of and increasingly willing to challenge or criticise central government policies and decisions. It is understood that quite a few Ministers at the time were less than thrilled with the proposals made by the colloquium in 2013 to effectively remove some powers from Ministers and transfer them to a Dublin mayor (Beesley, 2014; Kelly, 2014). We have by common consensus an executive-dominated system of government at national level. The fifteen cabinet Ministers that meet weekly hold the power of initiative, and if they can command a relatively stable majority in the Oireachtas, can ensure most bills pass into law with relative ease. There is little in the way of checks and balances between cabinet on the one hand, and the legislature, or indeed the Presidency on the other. Equally, local government's role in Ireland is modest in comparative terms. In short, there is little in the way of past history of Irish governments consciously establishing political offices that could act as a rival or counterbalance to the influence of cabinet, or a more vocal platform for potential future political adversaries.

Secondly, opposition has come from many backbench Oireachtas members fearful of the prospect of directly elected mayors as potential electoral rivals in future general elections. It was through pressure from backbench TDs in particular (rather than councillors) that forced the 2003 amendment of the Local Government Act, 2001 to revoke the provisions providing for directly elected mayors in each county and city council area. It seems that many backbench TDs and Senators at the time were less than comfortable about the prospect of political rivals from their area (including rivals within their own party) building up a significant local profile in their local constituencies by serving as directly elected mayor for a number of years.

Thirdly, opposition has come from within local government, and from many local councillors and chief executives who might see their role diminished through the creation of a new political figurehead for the local authority. International experience would suggest that the introduction of directly elected mayors can come at the expense of a reduced influence for the elected council, which can arguably represent a better cross-section of views and minority interests within an area. More immediately, some councillors have opposed the introduction of directly elected mayors because of a fear of 'celebrity' or single-issue candidates, or because such a position might deprive most councillors of the opportunity to hold office as mayor, as opposed to the current situation whereby the office is rotated between five councillors over the term of the council (Kenny, 2003). However, it may be that opposition from councillors has dissipated somewhat in recent years – a 2012 survey of local councillors suggested that 51% supported the idea, with 39% opposed (Government of Ireland 2012). As noted above, the majority of councillors in the Dublin local authorities in 2014 supported the idea of holding a plebiscite on whether to establish a directly elected mayor in Dublin (although some councillors emphasised at the time that they supported Dublin citizens having a vote on the matter, but were not necessarily supporting a directly elected mayor per se).

Lastly, one might also envisage a final hurdle to be crossed – whether citizens are likely to approve of the proposal to establish a directly elected mayor in any future plebiscite? As we know from our own history and from international experience, referendums can be somewhat unpredictable affairs. Polls that show strong support for a proposal early on in a referendum campaign are no guarantee that a proposal will pass. When citizens in a number of the larger cities in Britain were asked whether they thought a directly elected mayor should be established for their area, voters in many cities said 'no'. So, it seems that even if we got to the stage where a plebiscite was called on whether to establish a directly elected mayor in Dublin or elsewhere in Ireland, it is by no means a foregone conclusion that voters will back the idea.

CHAPTER 8
A DIRECTLY ELECTED MAYORAL MODEL OF GOVERNANCE FOR DUBLIN: CONSIDERATION OF SOME INTERNATIONAL EXAMPLES

Orla O'Donnell

Introduction

The development of a directly elected mayor model is comprehensively catalogued in a number of studies. Sadioglu and Dede (2016: xxiii) argue that in the 1990s the issue of leadership in terms of local government reform became more important and the main focus of this was a "stronger and directly elected mayor model" based on the idea that the mayor should be directly elected by the citizens and the mayor should play a strong role in the municipality administration. 'Strong leadership in local governments is undoubtedly related to other both input-oriented (for political legitimacy) and output oriented (for economic efficiency) reforms. For this reason, the directly elected mayor model was regarded as an important reform element completing new tools introduced with new public management, governance and direct democracy paradigms.' (Sadioglu and Dede, 2016: xxiii) But, Sadioglu and Dede found that produced results did not fully comply with the prior justifications suggested. An important point is raised by Keles (2016), where he stresses that although the European Charter of Local Self-Government does not require that the executive organ of local authorities to be directly elected by the people, the number of countries electing their mayors by direct popular vote grew considerably during the 1990s, as in Austria, Germany and Italy.

A strong mayoral system, where the executive is directly responsible to the voters, instead of the municipal council, is becoming more common all over Europe. Similarly, Pleschberger underlines that "the directly elected mayor is a prominent manifestation of global efforts to innovate and strengthen local democracy" (2016: 112). Pleschberger also highlights that according to the established reformist claim, a directly elected mayor generates an array of advantages for local democracy (e.g. personalisation, visibility of power, an increase in accountability, more inclusion, even direct involvement of citizens in local decision making). The model seems to overcome the democratic deficits of the indirectly elected mayor model; this is the core assumption of the "difference hypothesis" (2016: 110). Sweeting questions that:

> ... though mayors directly elected by the residents of a city are so commonplace as to go without comment in the United States and Canada, in many other countries, including England, Germany, and Hungary, they are a recent development, where they have been pitched as an effective, democratically accountable governing option, - is this proposition valid and do directly elected mayors deliver better governance than the alternatives? (2017: 1).

Similarly, Quinlivan (2008: 1) emphasises that Magre and Bertrana (2007: 181) refer to institutional reforms in local government in Western Europe as leading to significant changes in inter-organic relations and they examine the introduction, in some countries, of directly elected mayors (England, Germany, Italy, Austria, Greece and Portugal) towards institutional convergence in the aforementioned countries.

The historical development of propositions for a directly elected mayor in an Irish context will be lightly discussed in this chapter at the outset, but, the focus of this chapter is on the development of a directly elected mayoral model in terms of providing opportunities for strategic collaboration. It should also be noted that there is a range of mayoral models in existence. The examples from the international literature reviewed in this chapter provide insights along this continuum and allow us to consider the implications of a directly elected mayor model in terms of greater development of strategic collaborations. Section two of this chapter examines the rationale for types of mayoral governance and strategic collaboration. Section three sets out international examples of mayoral initiatives. The international examples in particular provide useful insights. The chapter highlights an array of options for developing a directly elected mayoral model of governance in the Capital City to provide greater strategic direction and to enhance co-operation and collaboration across organisations and jurisdictional lines.

Rationale for Strategic Collaboration
Strategic collaboration is defined by Norris-Tirrell and Clay (2010: 2) as "an intentional, collective approach to address public problems or

issues through building shared knowledge, designing innovative solutions, and forging consequential change". They note that "when used strategically, collaboration produces positive impacts, stakeholders committed to policy or programme change, and strengthened capacity of individuals and organisations to effectively work together." While it is noted that resource sharing is not a new concept as local government organisations have been working together and sharing resources for many years, at a time of fiscal challenge such as the present it is useful to think in terms of developing a governance model that engenders greater strategic collaboration. A directly elected Mayoral model for our Capital City is seen as a possible opportunity to galvanise these collaborative efforts at local government level.

Given the current economic climate of limited resources, increasing demands on services and complex community expectations, it is important that councils look at strategic collaborations and partnerships as ways to respond to these challenges. Norris-Tirrell and Clay (2010: 2) emphasise that almost any problem today is too complex to be addressed individually or by organisations working alone in their silos: 'What in the past would have appeared as a straight forward administrative problem now more than not requires working with other programmes, agencies, citizens, and multiple stakeholders across policy arenas.' They further note that public and non-profit administrators often stumble into collaboration without a strategic orientation:

For example, a governor or mayor forms an interagency collaboration on infant mortality, sustainability, workforce development, or the "current topic of the day" to make innovative recommendations; however, conveners fail to proactively establish a strategic agenda around the collaboration. Thus the group remains in their comfortable discipline or agency silos and produce limited results. Unquestionably, collaboration is a useful tool, but, one that we argue needs to be used with more intentionality, as public and non-profit administrators wrestle with skilfully engaging in and facilitating collaborative structures, processes, and outcomes (Norris-Tirrell and Clay (2010: xi).

Furthermore, Bryson, Crosby and Middleton Stone (2006: 44) highlight that cross-sector collaboration occurs for many reasons. "The first is simply that we live in a shared-power world in which many groups and organisations are involved in, affected by, or have some partial responsibility to act on public challenges". Beyond that, in the United States, advocates of power sharing across sectors are often responding to a long-standing critique of the effectiveness of government when it acts on its own (Crosby and Bryson, 2005).

The New South Wales Department of Local Government's Guidance Paper on Collaboration and Partnerships between Councils suggests that "strategic collaboration is where councils enter into arrangements with each other for mutual benefit" (2007: 6). The guidance paper also emphasises that strategic collaboration is an umbrella term for how councils work together and that it can take many forms including alliances, partnerships, business clusters, and so on. The paper points out that the purpose of strategic collaboration is to reduce duplication of services, provide cost savings, access innovation, enhance skills development and open the way for local communities to share ideas and connect with others. Strategic collaboration offers participating councils a way to achieve their goals and objectives in cost effective and innovative ways.

Bryson, Crosby and Middleton Stone (2006: 45) emphasise that the perceived need to collaborate across sectors has provoked two general responses. 'On the one hand, our own view is that organisational participants in effective cross-sector collaborations typically have to fail into their role in the collaboration. In other words, organisations will only collaborate when they cannot get what they want without collaborating (Hudson et al., 1999; Roberts, 2001). The second response is to assume that collaboration is the Holy Grail of solutions and always best. Often, governments and foundations insist that funding recipients collaborate, even if they have little evidence that it will work (Barringer and Harrison, 2000; Ostrower, 2005). Similarly, Norris-Tirrell and Clay (2010:73) outline that moving from silos to collaboration requires public and non-profit managers to think differently about working beyond discipline, organisation, and sector boundaries.

As depicted by Norris-Tirrell and Clay (2010: 4) in figure 8.1 below, collaborative activity, as previously noted, falls on a continuum:

> On the far left of the continuum are pure silo-based activities, where issues are seen as solely and appropriately placed with the agency. As boundary-spanning functions increase in magnitude, the activities

move to the right along the collaborative continuum, from simple collaborative activities to full-blown strategic collaboration. The issues at hand may require only minimal level of collaboration that is more short-term in nature and simpler in its purpose. In contrast, thorny problems that are interconnected with other policy arenas and have high investment on the part of other agencies, sectors, and interests may require a strategic approach to forming and building collaboration. All too often, decisions about building or joining a collaboration are not strategic in nature and lead to what can be labelled ad hoc collaboration...This common approach mirrors the notion of "muddling through" and "hoping for the best."...Unfortunately, collaborative inertia, fatigue, and frustration are the more likely outcomes from this non-strategic approach...To advance public service practice and reach long term solutions, collaborative activity needs to be appreciably more strategic in its approach to assure intentional, systematic, and inclusionary collaboration, as public and non-profit managers wrestle with trying to manage upward, downward, and outward within their particular context

Networking, Informal cooperation	Formal cooperation knowledge sharing, contracting	Transfer of functions, integration consolidation

Simple   Complex

Figure 8.1: Collaboration Continuum

Source: Norris-Tirrell and Clay (2010: 4).

Given the recent austerity measures, there has been a reduction in budgetary allocations to local authorities in many countries. There is a greater focus on collaborations, partnerships and outsourcing as a means to cut costs, improve efficiency and productivity. For example, Jepp (2011) highlights that in the UK, Swansea County Council plans to outsource almost all of its services in order to cut its £1.1billion budget by 30%. Kent and Reigate plan to save £4m through collaborating or linking up on four services (personnel, finance, benefits and revenues and IT). Suffolk County Council is outsourcing adult social services in a £20m per annum plan.

Jepp (2011) also emphasises that in the UK as the government continues to make changes to reduce the public deficit, "it is likely that the number of local authorities embarking on new and different relationships will rise – along with the breadth of risks they face. If these partnerships are undertaken without proper commissioning and risk management skills, there is every likelihood that costs will rise and service quality will decrease". Jepp also notes that recent research conducted highlights that only 29% of public sector leaders felt they were able to deal with the kinds of risks associated with working with other organisations (Tough Choices Report, 2011).

In many instances, intergovernmental collaboration allows localities to achieve better results than they could by working alone. A 1994 study of more than 50 instances of community collaboration found that successful collaborations have four major outcomes: they achieve tangible results, generate new processes that lead to solutions where traditional approaches have failed, empower residents and groups, and fundamentally change the way communities deal with complex issues. (NLC, 2006: 5-6). It is important to address whether or not organisations have the capabilities (time, staff, finances, structure) to fulfil their end of the agreement. Jepp (2011) notes that "it remains to be seen whether outsourcing and partnership working will bring the benefits local authorities hope, and many of the details and legalities have still to be determined. However, risk management should remain a top focus for local authorities." A directly elected mayor could be a useful resource to public sector leaders in managing some of these risks associated with collaborations.

Why do we need a Directly Elected Mayor When Existing Structures Are Collaborating on Socio-economic Projects?

In June, 2003, the Dublin City Development Board and Dublin Community Forum organised a well-attended "public trial" (chaired by Vincent Browne) on the topic of directly-elected mayors. All eight members of the jury panel voted for directly elected mayors and a straw poll of the audience at the end of the trial, recorded 59% voted for directly elected mayors. Prior to this event, a straw poll had been conducted of 600 members of the public on Grafton Street, asking them if they felt the Lord Mayor of Dublin should be elected by public vote or by the elected members of City Council? While such polls have limited scientific value, there was a clear majority in favour of the idea. Of these, however, only 55% felt that the Lord Mayor should have decision-making powers and 40% thought the mayor should be a figurehead for the City (Callanan, 2003).

A number of options were put forward by Byrne (2013) and discussed by a steering committee for a colloquium on 29th August 2013:

- Option 1: Directly Elected Executive Mayor;
- Option 2: Directly Elected Mayor/cabinet (collaborative) model;
- Option 3: Representational Directly Elected Mayor.

These 3 options are based on international examples of Mayoral Governance: UK Model, German Model and USA Model (see Byrne, 2013).

A private member's bill proposed a directly elected mayor of Dublin and head of a new regional authority for the City in 2016. The proposal suggested that a new Regional Authority and an office of the directly elected mayor would sit above the existing four Dublin Local Authorities in co-ordinating and leadership role within certain defined strategic policy areas: land-use planning; transport; waste management; water services. The new authority and office of the directly elected mayor would work through and with existing local government structures.

Existing Collaboration Mechanisms

Local Community Development Committees (LCDC) were created in each of the four local authorities in the Dublin region to bring together local authority members and officials, representatives from State agencies, the relevant local development companies and the Public Participation Network (PPN), for the purposes of developing, coordinating and implementing a coherent and integrated approach to local and community development in the County. The LCDC and Economic Development Strategic Policy Committee (SPC) prepared the Local Economic and Community Plans 2016-2021 in each of the local authority areas: to set out, for a six-year period, the objectives and actions needed to promote and support the local economic and community development of the relevant local authority area; both by itself directly and in partnership with other economic and community development stakeholders.

As structures of collaboration currently exist in each of the four local authority areas (LCDCs, SPC and CPGs and PPNs), does the proposal for a directly elected mayor need to be questioned? It is suggested in the literature that a directly elected mayor would bring a greater emphasis on strategic collaboration. It is proposed that the directly elected mayor and the new regional authority will be working with and through the four Dublin Local Authorities (officials and councillors; LCDCs, SPCs, civil society organisations and public sector agencies) to create greater focus and drive key strategic issues. In international examples, a directly elected mayor is seen as a key touchstone for big business to strategically collaborate with various interest groups on large projects (e.g. Weston development in Toronto).

Norris-Tirrell and Clay emphasise that almost any problem today is too complex to be addressed individually or by organisations working alone in their silos: "What in the past would have appeared as a straight forward administrative problem; now more than not requires working with other programmes, agencies, citizens, and multiple stakeholders across policy arenas" (2010: 2). Strategic collaboration is defined as "an intentional, collective approach to address public problems or issues through building shared knowledge, designing innovative solutions, and forging consequential change" (2010: 3). When used strategically, collaboration produces positive impacts, stakeholders committed to policy or programme change, and strengthened capacity of individuals and organisations to effectively work together.' Specifically, Norris-Tirrell and Clay stress that:

> For example, a governor or mayor forms an interagency collaboration on infant mortality, sustainability, workforce development, or the 'current topic of the day' to make innovative recommendations; however, conveners fail to proactively establish a strategic agenda around the collaboration. Thus the group remains in their comfortable discipline or agency silos and produces limited results... Unquestionably, collaboration is a useful tool, but, one that we argue needs to be used with

more intentionality, as public and non-profit administrators wrestle with skilfully engaging in and facilitating collaborative structures, processes, and outcomes (2010: xi).

Travers argues that "it is possible to add directly elected executive mayors into a very different (democratically conservative) system. London and other British local authorities have generally prospered, but, it is hard to 'prove' the benefits" (2011: 4). He notes that mayors have generally been popular where introduced and it is becoming a trend as a number of cities are introducing this type of office. To provide some empirical evidence to the discussion, Jesus Garcia and Sancino (2016) compared the Italian and Spanish case, discussing the influence of having elected or appointed mayors on local government systems. Their comparative analysis highlights that overall directly elected mayors have ensured better efficiency in terms of quicker provision of decision-making processes, even if mostly at the expense of democratic representation. Having direct or appointed mayors also impacted on accountability and legitimacy patterns. However, all these effects depended not only on other mechanisms, such as, for example, the strong majority prize provided by the electoral law and the bond of coexistence between the mayor and the council. Similarly, Pleschberger, 2016 analysed the democratic orientation and styles of actions of the indirectly elected mayors in the city of Vienna from 1973 to 2013 and the citizenry were asked to express their opinion in consultative referenda. The longitudinal study shows the clear preference of the mayors for representative democracy and the majority principle to decide local issues. The analysis provided evidence that indirectly supports the reformist claim promoting the directly elected mayoral model in local democracy.

In an Irish context, there are a number of recent examples cited by politicians for creating a Dublin mayoral office. For instance, the recent National Transport Authority (NTA) and Dublin City Council disagreement over NTA wanting to build an eastern by-pass across Dublin to complete the M50 ring road. But, Dublin City councillors voted to remove this from the development plan, urging a greater focus on public transport. But this removal was called into question by the City Council Executive as to its legality. Another example is the Web Summit, which in 2015 moved to Lisbon due to issues of networked infrastructure and transport access. Who is in charge of resolving these types of disputes? It is believed that a Directly Elected Mayor with overriding powers and strategic leadership would help overcome these types of issues. A directly elected mayor could use his or her role to develop investment opportunities and greater collaborative projects between the public and private sector investors and organisations.

International Examples

In this section of the chapter, some directly elected mayoralty-led strategic collaboration projects (involving communities) are reviewed from the international literature (for example, by Mayors in London, Toronto, Los Angeles, New York, and San Francisco).

<u>London</u>

Londoners voted in a referendum in 1998 to create new governance structures for Greater London. A directly elected mayor of Greater London was created in 2000. The first mayor elected was Ken Livingstone from 2000-2008; Boris Johnston was elected Mayor in 2008-2016 and Sadiq Khan is the current mayor and was elected in May 2016. It is a fixed four-year term and the current mayor may opt for re-election. Most powers are derived from the Greater London Authority Act, 1999 with additional functions coming from the Greater London Authority Act, 2007, the Localism Act, 2011 and Police Reform and Social Responsibility, Act 2011. The High Street Fund was launched in March 2015 to re-energise London's high streets by embracing the City's talent for creativity and innovation. It is the first time a mayor of any major European City has used civic crowdfunding website (Spacehive) to directly pledge money to community projects[32].

Culture on the High Street (July 2013) highlights some of the ways which councils, high street and town centre teams are collaborating with artists and the creative community to create better and distinctive places. The Mayor's 'Pocket Park' initiative is to create 100 mini-oases (£2m investment from City Hall) by transforming public places (high streets, town centres, parks, rivers and pathways) into vibrant loved places within the City, delivered by Groundwork on behalf of the

---

[32] Spacehive a web portal where community groups are able to post their ideas and ask for financial support, see http://www.london.gov.uk/highstreetfund and http://spacehive.com/Initiatives/mayoroflondon for more details.

Mayor to build on the work of Groundwork's Transform initiative which began as a key part of the London 2012 Changing Places programme and has already forged close links with local partners. For example, the 'Pocket Park' initiative is part of the Mayor's London Great Outdoors programme and since the programme began in 2009, over £250m has been invested in over 78 projects, divided into two key areas – better green and water spaces and better streets[33].

On 16th August 2016, the new Mayor of London Sadiq Khan marked 100 days in office and spoke about big changes that were required in important areas, such as, housing, transport, culture, skills and equality. The Mayor highlighted a numbers of milestones achieved in 100 days:

- The London Night Tube service running;
- Announced a Transport for London (TfL) fares freeze for 4 years and announced a Hopper bus fare (2 bus journeys in an hour for the price of one anywhere in London);
- Blocked plans to develop on London's green space;
- Created a Homes for Londoners team to ensure genuinely affordable homes to rent and buy;
- Focus on real neighbourhood policing with an extra police officer in every ward by 2017;
- Put together ambitious plan to tackle air pollution in London;
- Working on plans for London's first cultural enterprise zone to support arts and culture;
- Published the first gender pay audit at City Hall and a plan to tackle pay inequality.

Quinlivan (2008: 9) highlights that "the one lesson Ireland can learn from the United Kingdom is that it is essential to create a clear, unambiguous mayoral model" as the UK had offered too many options and suffered from a "double-handicap" as the office of city/county manager did not previously exist. Quinlivan (2008: 9) further outlines that 'the main lesson to be learned from the United States is the

---

[33] See http://www.London.gov.uk/greatoutdoors, https://www.groundwork. org.uk /sites/london and https://www.london.gov.uk/what-we-do/ enviro-nment/parks-green-spaces-and-biodiversity/pocket-parks-project for details.

importance of clarifying relationships. This is clearly evident in the example of the Vision Zero Project summarised below.

Vision Zero Network

Collaborating across departments to achieve Vision Zero (2016) highlights some useful examples in terms of the instrumental work that can be achieved by cross-collaboration between mayors, political authorities, city organisations and local communities around key policy issues and goals. From the perspective of the Vision Zero Network the primary mission of government is to protect the public and the network leads a campaign to achieve zero traffic fatalities on city streets.

The chapter highlights a number of USA examples that detail specific ways Vision Zero cities are restructuring their collaboration in long-lasting ways to take meaningful action for safe streets. One of the defining characteristics of Vision Zero is the key focus on breaking down silos and uniting local stakeholders around common goals. Cross-departmental collaboration is a critical basis to a successful Vision Zero commitment. Cities like San Francisco, Los Angeles, Washington, D.C. and New York City have developed ways to bridge unintentional, but, long-standing gaps between key local agencies and identified innovative means to build new organisational architecture to advance Vision Zero.

The mayor played a critical role in committing a community to Vision Zero as a top priority of his or her administration but once that commitment is made, many mayors have invested resources from their office to mobilise the right agencies and top leaders within the city to activate things in a meaningful way. In New York City, immediately after the release of the Vision Zero Action Plan in February 2014, Mayor Bill de Blasio's Office of Operations held a meeting at City Hall with agency heads to set out the framework for the permanent Vision Zero Taskforce, as well as to identify agency leads to participate. But de Blasio didn't delegate the work, since its inception the Mayor's Office of Operations (Ops) has been the primary convener and consistent catalyst of the Vision Zero initiative. Key city agencies (including transportation, police, health and the mayor's office) appointed by the mayor to lead the strategy and implementation of Vision Zero. The NYC Vision Zero Taskforce includes the Police Department, Department of Transportation, Taxi and Limousine Commission, Department of Health and Mental Hygiene, Department of Citywide Administrative Services, Law Department and Office of Management and Budget. In Los Angeles, the Mayor appointed the General Manager of the Department of Transportation and the Chief of Police (or their designates) as co-chairs of the Vision Zero Executive Steering Committee. In Washington, the Mayor tapped the Department of Transportation as the lead agency on the Vision Zero Taskforce. Many cities engage community stakeholders in their Taskforces in some way.

In San Francisco, when Vision Zero was first launched in 2014, Mayor Ed Lee's office assigned a dedicated, full-time staff member to assist with convening and mobilising the city's Vision Zero Taskforce. To ensure the initiative became integral to department operations, that taskforce is staffed with senior city leaders including the Director of Sustainable Streets at the Municipal Transportation Agency; the Director of the Programme on Health, Equity and Sustainability at the Department of Public Health; and Traffic Commander at the San Francisco Police Department. San Francisco released an Action Strategy in 2015 and releases a quarterly progress report to coincide with the quarterly Taskforce and Vision Zero Committee meetings, which collectively aims to improve transparency and accountability. The Vision Zero SF Two-Year Action Strategy outlines the projects and policy changes the City plans to pursue in the next two years to build safety and liveability into city streets. The Action Strategy encompasses a range of solutions to address street safety comprehensively and citywide that will bring us closer to achieving the Vision Zero goal of zero deaths on City streets by 2024 (Vision Zero, 2017).

Multiple City departments will collaborate to achieve this ambitious agenda over the next two years. The goal was to create measurable progress by the end of 2016 and initiate future strategies in two-year increments that focus on reaching the City's policy goal to save lives and reduce serious injuries. The Mayor provides the strategic leadership when he commits the city to Vision Zero and plays a key role in managing the process to achieve it. Shared goals and inter-agency conversations through cross-sectoral collaboration (taskforces/sub-committees). Community involvement in these committees and taskforce. Regular meetings and tracking progress ensures data is used to drive collaboration. Joint funding and budgeting can also unite departments behind a common goal, as in the case of Vision Zero. In addition to data, dollars are an essential asset to advance Vision Zero, not just in funding projects and programmes, budgeting can also unite departments behind a common goal. It can also lead to innovation, for example, through Vision Zero a new transportation database was created in Los Angeles.

New York

One of the central ways to cross-departmental collaboration is the formation of a strong, committed taskforce that comprises the right stakeholders meeting on an organised, consistent basis. The makeup of such taskforces (or steering committees) vary by community but representation from four key areas is critical: the Mayor's office, the Department of Transportation, the Police Department and Public Health Department. Ensuring management-level staff participation from various city departments is also essential to galvanise the buy-in and action necessary to achieve Vision Zero goals. In New York City, the taskforce is "led" by three agencies — the NYC Police Department, Department of Transportation, and the Taxi and Limousine Commission — but also includes the Department of Health and Mental Hygiene, Department of Citywide Administrative Services, the Law Department and the Office of Management and Budget, along with representatives from the District Attorney's Offices and the Metropolitan Transportation Authority. In many ways, the taskforce is the hub of the multi-agency effort. It provides a structure to create common goals, share ideas and strategies, problem-solve barriers and build inter-agency trust and new personal relationships, the taskforce has the ability — and responsibility — to shift the city's fundamental approach to traffic safety in a profound way. But these groups aren't limited to city government. Many communities also engage advocacy organisations and community stakeholders in their taskforces. While the taskforce provides essential leadership, many communities have established subcommittees — or working groups — to delve deeper into the areas most critical to Vision Zero. These subcommittees not only examine important issues, like data collection or engineering, but also provide opportunities for further cross-departmental collaboration and action by convening additional interdisciplinary discussions.

Los Angeles

In Los Angeles, for instance, the full taskforce is divided into four subcommittees, each aligning with one of the key Vision Zero Issue Areas: Engineering, Enforcement, Education, and Evaluation. Each subcommittee has an assigned chair who is responsible for convening and reporting on clear Executive Directive Action Items, a model practice that lends more accountability and transparency to the work.

San Francisco

San Francisco has a similar approach. Tom Maguire, Director of Sustainable Streets at the San Francisco Municipal Transportation Agency states that "There are six standing committees — Engineering, Enforcement, Education, Policy, Evaluation, and Budget. Some meet regularly, while others convene on an ad hoc basis. The six committee chairs meet bi-weekly as the Vision Zero Core Group, which I chair."

In New York City, working groups on Marketing and Data respectively have had a big impact. Geraldine Sweeney, Chief Strategy Advisor in the Mayor's Office of Operations states that:

> We have found these to be highly collaborative, producing some innovative deliverables including the Vision Zero View map, an interactive tool that shows detailed information on traffic injury and fatality crashes in New York City and highlights how the City is responding every day to make our streets safer. Another key deliverable from the Marketing Working Group is the interagency marketing plan and unified budget which outlined an educational and marketing strategy to allow us to reach key target audiences effectively. This plan outlines how we will collectively and successfully market the Vision Zero brand and its objectives. And in doing so ensures that all agencies are speaking with one voice (2016: 4).

Toronto

The Mayor of Toronto is directly elected for a four-year term and may opt for re-election. The City of Toronto Act, 2006 sets out the role of the Mayor as the head of council as follows:

- Act as chief executive officer;
- Provide information and make recommendations to Council with respect to Council's role in ensuring that administrative policies, practices and procedures and controllership policies, practices and procedures are in place to implement the decisions of Council and in ensuring the accountability and transparency of the operations of the City, including the activities of the senior management of the City;
- Preside over (chairs) meetings of council so that its business can be carried out efficiently and effectively;
- Provide leadership to council;
- Represent the City at official functions, and carry out any other duties under the City of Toronto Act, 2006 or any other Act.

Eleven committees report to Toronto City Council. The Mayor is a member of all committees and is entitled to one vote. The Executive Committee is an advisory body chaired by the mayor. The Executive Committee is composed of the Mayor, Deputy Mayor, and the chairs of the seven standing committees who are appointed by the Mayor and four members appointed by City Council. The role of the Executive Committee is to set the City of Toronto's priorities, manage financial planning and budgeting, labour relations, human resources, and the operation of City Council. The Executive Committee makes recommendations to city council on: strategic policy and priorities; governance policy and structure; financial planning and budgeting; fiscal policy (revenue and tax policies); intergovernmental and international relations; Council operations; human resources and labour relations. Several committees report to the Executive Committee: Budget Committee; Affordable Housing Committee, and Employee and Labour Relations Committee.

On 22nd June 2016, Mayor John Tory joined a coalition of partners and Weston community members to announce a vibrant new community development in Toronto's Weston neighbourhood. The ground was broken for a planned transition of the site-currently a parking lot and an adjacent high rise between King and John Streets into a mixed use development (incorporates housing, arts and community spaces and a farmers' market). Weston has been identified by the City of Toronto as a Neighbourhood Improvement Area.

Partners in the redevelopment include Rockport Group, the Toronto Parking Authority (TPA), Artscape and Woodbourne Capital Management. For the Toronto Parking Authority, the project is the first that encompasses its newly adopted Community Benefits Policy, which states that the TPA incorporate community benefits whenever establishing, refurbishing or redeveloping its off-street parking facilities. The Weston community development will include, 8,200 square feet dedicated to arts, cultural and community events programming; 370 apartment units, including six affordable rental homes; 12,400 square feet of outdoor publicly accessible space for community gatherings and farmers markets; and 26 affordable live/work units for artist-led families.

Mayor Tory outlined at the launch that "through this public-private partnership, residents are going to get a complete neighbourhood with mixed housing, public space for farmers markets, and space dedicated for arts and cultural events" (2016: 3). The City Council of Toronto stated that it is the first private investment of its type in Weston in 40 years. In January 2015, Mayor John Tory established the Mayor's Taskforce on Toronto Community Housing, led by former City of Toronto Mayor, Senator Art Eggleton. An independent six-person Housing Taskforce was appointed to take a hard look at how Toronto Community Housing serves the people of Toronto and how it is governed. The Taskforce was asked to offer advice on how to strengthen and support the delivery of housing to Toronto Community Housing residents in the areas of operations and delivery, partnerships and innovation, capital revitalisation and new development, and governance. The Taskforce held five public meetings to hear from Toronto Community Housing residents. On 15th July 2015, the Taskforce submitted an interim report to Mayor Tory entitled Improved Living at Toronto Community Housing: Priority Action. The Taskforce called on Toronto Community Housing to develop action plans within 60 days to address immediate concerns identified by residents in four key areas: safety and security, building conditions, jobs and opportunities for residents, and training for staff and contractors.

Toronto Community Housing presented its action plans, entitled Getting it done: Real change at Toronto Community Housing, to Mayor Tory and the Taskforce on 10th September 2015. The action plans included work that was already underway or planned, plus additional work that could be prioritised immediately or in the short term to bring about sustained positive changes for the benefit of residents. The Taskforce delivered a Final Report in January 2016. The final report was tabled by the Mayor at the 28th January 2016 Executive Committee. The Committee unanimously voted to refer the report to the City Manager for an initial assessment of the recommendations and underlying assumptions and principles. Of the 71 specific projects in the report, 32 were to be completed in 2015 and 19 in 2016. The remaining 20 projects could not be carried out under Toronto Community Housing's current budget and would require additional funding from the City or through partnerships. Bryson, Crosby and Middleton Stone note that cross-sector collaboration occurs for many reasons:

The first is simply that we live in a shared-power world in which many groups and organisations are involved in, affected by, or have some partial responsibility to act on public challenges. Beyond that, in the United States, advocates of power sharing across sectors are often responding to a long-standing critique of the effectiveness of government when it acts on its own (2006: 44).

Conclusion

This chapter has reviewed a number of examples of Mayoral models which are encouraging greater co-operation and collaboration across organisations and regions. Ultimately, as the National League of Cities (NLC) Guide to Successful Local Government Collaboration in America's Regions (2006) argues it is about making strategic collaboration the norm and from the international examples reviewed in this chapter, it can be seen that having a directly elected Mayor in a City seems to bring to fruition a greater number of strategic cross-collaborative projects. It is about collaborating across jurisdictional lines becomes the expected approach in dealing with complex issues, not just a one-time event, and becomes a natural ingredient in any manager's set of capabilities. The NLC guide emphasises that collaborations are based on an understanding among leaders and residents alike that challenges facing communities and regions require a crossing of multiple boundaries, including political, geographic, economic, racial, and ethnic (NLC, 2006: 53). The international examples reviewed in this chapter, highlight that a directly elected mayor provides the strategic leadership to create that space between the various players.

Norris-Tirrell and Clay (2010: 314) suggest that strategic collaboration offers an increased likelihood of success and positive outcomes from the collaborative venture as public and non-profit managers become more purposeful about collaboration design and implementation processes, enable collaboration inclusiveness and effectiveness, decrease collaboration fatigue and frustrations, and proactively steer toward positive outcomes. Similarly, NLC's report provide a series of steps and tools to assist councils develop effective collaborative arrangements. Bryson, Crosby and Middleton Stone (2006: 52) emphasise that success in cross-sector collaborations depends on leadership of many different kinds and they highlight leadership roles "such as sponsors, champions, boundary spanners, and facilitators". But, Huxham and Vangen (2005: 202-212) argue that leadership – in the sense of what "makes things happen" - also occurs through structures and processes. Therefore, the leadership challenge in cross-sector collaboration may be viewed as a challenge of aligning initial conditions, processes, structures, governance, contingencies and constraints, outcomes, and accountabilities such that good things happen in a sustained way over time-indeed, so that public value can be created.

As noted in the international literature, and underlined by Pleschberger (2016) the directly elected mayor is a prominent manifestation of global efforts to innovate and strengthen local democracy. Pleschberger explains that the established reformist claim, that a directly elected mayor "generates an array of advantages for local democracy, e.g. personalisation, visibility of power, an increase in accountability, more inclusion, even direct involvement of citizens in local decision making" (2016: 112). The directly elected mayor model seems to overcome the democratic deficits of the indirectly elected mayor model.

This chapter has reviewed a number of examples of mayoral models which encourage greater co-operation and collaboration across organisations and regions. Ultimately, as the NLC argues it is about making strategic collaboration the norm and from the international examples reviewed in this chapter, it can be seen that having a directly elected mayor in a city seems to bring to fruition a greater number of strategic cross-collaborative projects. It is about collaborating across jurisdictional lines becoming the expected approach in dealing with complex issues, not just a one-time event and becoming a natural ingredient in any manager's set of capabilities. The international examples reviewed in this chapter, highlight that a directly elected mayor provides the strategic leadership to create that space for constructive interaction between the various players.

As has been highlighted by the international examples, a directly elected mayor provides the vital touchstone to harness the potential benefits of cross-sectoral collaborations around agreed policy areas and secure public-private sector investment in necessary infrastructure projects through cross-sectoral taskforces and subcommittees developing innovative structures and processes between international organisations, local authorities, philanthropic and voluntary organisations in the relevant cities.

CHAPTER 9
IS IRELAND READY FOR DIRECTLY ELECTED MAYORS? JUST DO IT!

Aodh Quinlavin

Introduction

Popular discourse in Ireland is sometimes obsessed with micro-level debates on structure and form to such an extent that the bigger macro level issues are missed.

Accordingly, the public sector reform strategy of 2011 was about shedding 40,000 people and the local government reform strategy of Minister Phil Hogan TD was about reducing the number of local authorities from 114 to 31. The rhetoric in both cases was all about rationalisation, efficiencies and economies of scale. At no point, were more fundamental questions asked, such as:

- What do citizens want from our public sector?
- What kind of local government system do Irish people want in 21st century Ireland?
- What services should that local government system be providing?
- What is the role of the state?
- What is the optimal scale and scope of government?

Providing answers to these questions may facilitate structures to follow more naturally.

Essentially there is a need to establish basic first principles. 25 years ago, in the author's first class on local government in University College Cork with Dick Haslam, the former Limerick County Manager, he told the class that local government exists for two fundamental reasons:

- As a local provider of public services;
- As a democratic counter-poise to central government domination.

Dick Haslam argued that it was a dangerous thing if one of these objectives overshadowed the other. If we focus entirely on efficiencies and economies of scale we run the risk of destroying the democratic legitimacy of local government.

In organisational studies and indeed in fields like modernist architecture and industrial design there are ongoing debates about whether form should follow function and this is a pertinent debate too for local government to have.

Altering the structure of local governance will not, in of itself, fix the weaknesses inherent in the Irish sub-national system. If there is a genuine will to reform local government, a holistic approach is needed, encompassing discussions on constitutional protection, functions, powers, finance, as well as capacity and competency requirements.

In 1982, a book written by Tom Peters and Richard Waterman was published, entitled In Search of Excellence and quickly became a best-seller. This was a management book which explored the traits of successful companies who continually exhibited innovation and returned healthy profits annually. Surprisingly, for a somewhat dry text on management, it was the most widely held library book in the United States between 1989 and 2006. Local government in Ireland and public sector management has not focused enough on 'excellence' rather 'in search of mediocrity' would be a more accurate description. The famous work of Professor Charles Lindblom in 1959 entitled, 'The Science of Muddling Through', perhaps not surprisingly, his follow-up article 20 years later bore the title, 'Still Muddling, not yet Through' provides an excellent description of local government in Ireland, it remains very muddled, with ad-hoc and inconsistent reform efforts every few years.

If Ireland is ever to adopt a holistic approach to local government reform there should of course be room to discuss governance structures and, for example, moving towards a model of directly elected mayors. Interestingly, the issue of directly elected mayors and our treatment of that issue is symbolic of our general approach to local government reform.

- The Local Government Act, 2001 said we would have directly elected mayors starting in 2004;
- The Local Government Act, 2003 said, 'no, we won't';
- Minister John Gormley's White Paper of 2008 said we would have a directly elected mayor for Dublin starting on 2011;
- It didn't happen.

- In the 2014 Act, Minister Phil Hogan provided for a directly elected mayor in Dublin but bizarrely inserted a road-block that all four Dublin local authorities would individually have to adopt a resolution in favour of holding a plebiscite.
- Fingal County Council blocked the initiative and it is now, temporarily at least, dead in the water.

What is it exactly that we are trying to achieve? Do we have a coherent plan or are we muddling through? To paraphrase Lewis Carroll from Alice in Wonderland, 'If you don't know where you're going, any road will take you there.'

The former Dublin City Manager, John Tierney, has argued that grafting a directly elected mayor onto the current system, without any meaningful changes to local government responsibilities and financing, will not make any appreciable difference. This supports the argument previously put forward by Colin Copus's contribution to this volume that the elected mayoral model has struggled in the UK due to the lack of power and meaning of local government.

We can point to certain international trends with regard to local governance. For example, there is little doubt that the strengthening of executive leadership at local level is an enduring theme. This is often manifested through a model of strong directly elected mayors. Countries with directly elected mayors are now the biggest group within Europe, with the number growing significantly in the 1990s.

But are there other trends? In the United States, the mayoral model is in decline and the proportion of US local authorities using the council-manager system has risen from a third to a half over the past 25 years.

Professor Copus has discussed the UK experience with directly elected mayors but it does appear that the public has not taken to the concept, although this does not make it a bad idea. The Conservative/Liberal Democrats coalition government initiated 10 mayoral referendums in selected English cities in 2012. Only in one did the people decide to establish the office of mayor – in Bristol on a 24% turnout.

Fenwick and Elcock concluded,

> Overall, there is no evidence of widespread public support for mayors, yet the prospect of more mayors –

indeed, mayors with enhanced powers – remains firmly on the policy agenda. This is interesting but also puzzling. A major continuing policy initiative is built on few empirical foundations (2014a: 2).

There is a lot of merit in the concept of directly elected mayors. It can also be argued that Dublin does warrant its own local governance structures due to its special position within Ireland. As Jamie Cudden wrote in a special issue of the journal Administration, "the future will be won or lost in the world's cities" (2015: 150).

Dublin can become an important hub in the global economy and it requires governance structures to support rather than hinder this aspiration. Harry McGee made the case for an elected mayor for Dublin. He argued, correctly in my view, "Dublin isn't competing with Limerick or Waterford. Its rivals include London, Paris, Berlin, Madrid and Barcelona. It's competing with them for investment, tourism and conferences" (McGee, 2016a).

The key sentence in his article however is the following: "The city needs an identifiable medium-term political leader who can speak on its behalf and will have powers to influence transport and traffic policy, sustainable transport, tourism, trade and economy, marketing, infrastructure and other services" (McGee, 2016a). It is hard to disagree with this sentence but given the fact that most of the powers McGee cites are currently outside the functional remit of Irish local government, he is proposing a radical shift in central-local relations.

Is there the political will to make this shift? It is unlikely that there is. Many are even more certain that the officials in the Custom House do not want to see this happen. Efforts over the past 15 years, briefly chronicled below, are telling (see Quinlivan 2015b for further details).

The Local Government Act, 2001 and the Introduction of Directly Elected Mayors

In the Local Government Act, 2001, under Minister Noel Dempsey TD, we actually passed legislation to introduce directly elected mayors. Section 40 of the legislation provided for the direct election of mayors, for a five-year term, with executive functions, to be effective from the following set of local elections in June 2004. The 2001 Act was noteworthy for its lack of detail about the precise functions of the mayor and how the office would impinge on the traditional role of the city/county manager (now called Chief Executive Officer). These issues were never clarified and, in a dramatic shifting of positions in 2003, the government repealed the directly elected mayor proposal from the 2001 Act.

In presenting the Local Government Bill to the Irish Senate on 26th February 2003, Minister Martin Cullen, TD, explained that he was planning major changes to the local government system. Once these changes had time to 'bed down', the issue of the mayor's election and role would be reconsidered.

At that point, the question as to whether Ireland should have directly elected mayors was put on hold but, in the build-up to the 2007 General Election, Green Party leader Trevor Sargent TD announced that his party, in government, would introduce directly elected mayors to make local government democratically accountable. The Fine Gael and Labour Party manifestos also contained a pledge to introduce directly elected mayors. Following the election, a coalition government was formed with Fianna Fáil, the Green Party and the Progressive Democrats. The three parties produced a programme for government which pledged to introduce a directly elected mayor for Dublin with executive powers by 2011. In addition, the government promised a Green Paper on Local Government Reform to address the issue of directly elected mayors.

In April 2008 the Minister for the Environment, Heritage and Local Government, John Gormley TD, published his promised Green Paper, entitled Stronger Local Democracy: Options for Change. Though the Green Paper was essentially a consultation document, it contained a useful and well-framed discussion of the directly elected mayor issue. The Green Paper favoured the introduction of a directly elected mayor not only for Dublin but also across the other city and county councils. With regards to Dublin, two main options were presented:

- A directly elected mayor for the existing Dublin City Council area;
- A 'city-region' mayor for the wider Dublin area.

The second option opened up a jurisdictional discussion about the wider Dublin area. Would Dublin have a regional mayor for the four local authorities – Dublin City Council, Fingal County Council, South Dublin County Council and Dún Laoghaire–Rathdown County Council

– or for a Greater Dublin Region incorporating Meath, Kildare and Wicklow? Ultimately, the Green Paper indicated a preference for an elected mayor for the four Dublin local authorities.

The paper then developed into a discussion on the different options with regard to mayoral powers, with examples drawn from New Zealand, Germany, Italy, the Netherlands, Sweden, Finland and England. Particular attention was paid to the London model, with the mayor having a limited set of strategic functions in areas such as transport, planning and economic development while the thirty-three London Borough Councils carried out their functions within the regional framework established by the mayor. Interestingly, the Green Paper suggested that different mayoral options could be applied in different areas or tested on a pilot basis. The Green Paper ultimately served its purpose in that it presented options for change and it did so in a thought-provoking manner. Alas, by the time the government left office nearly three years later, no White Paper had been produced and none of Minister Gormley's reform ideas had seen the legislative light of day.

It was a further three years before the issue of directly elected mayors came forward in legislation again. The Local Government Reform Act, 2014 received little media attention or public scrutiny in Ireland. However, the one issue to get pulses racing – at least in one part of the country – was the proposal in Part 11 to have a directly elected mayor for the Dublin Metropolitan Area. Minister Phil Hogan's legislation proposed the holding of a Dublin plebiscite on the issue on the same day as the 2014 local elections – 23 May. Controversially, however, the minister included a provision that each of the four local authorities which constitute the Dublin Metropolitan Area – Dublin City Council, Fingal County Council, South Dublin County Council and Dún Laoghaire–Rathdown County Council – would firstly have to individually adopt a resolution in favour of holding the plebiscite.

The insertion of this veto power for any one of the four Dublin local authorities was a curious move by the minister, and always had the potential to open up the proverbial can of worms. And so it proved. Three of the four Dublin local authorities comfortably adopted resolutions in favour of the plebiscite but, critically, the other local authority did not. The process began on Monday 24th March when Dublin City Council approved with fifty votes in favour and none against. One week later, on Monday 31st March, the remaining three councils met to decide the fate of the mayoral plebiscite. The vote in South Dublin County Council was nineteen in favour with three against; in Dún Laoghaire–Rathdown County Council, the elected members voted decisively in favour by twenty-three to zero.

The sting in the tail, however, was spectacularly delivered by the members of Fingal County Council, who voted against the holding of the plebiscite by sixteen votes to six. Accordingly, the proposal died and was not brought before the people of Dublin on 23rd May. Advocates of the directly elected mayor idea were appalled by the fact that the plebiscite had been blocked despite the overwhelming majority of councillors in Dublin voting in favour. The combined total vote was 98–19 and yet the minority of councillors against the proposal successfully rejected it. Rather than putting the decision to have a directly elected mayor in the hands of the citizens of Dublin, Minister Hogan placed an unnecessary obstacle into the process.

So why did Fingal County Council reject the proposal? Councillor Gerry McGuire of the Labour Party, one of those who voted against, argued that any directly elected mayor would be based in the city and would ignore rural Dublin, including the residents of Fingal. He added that the Local Government Reform Act, 2014 did not provide enough detail about the role and powers of the mayor and so people would not know precisely what they were voting on.

In essence, Minister Phil Hogan's 2014 plan for a directly elected mayor for the Dublin Metropolitan region, was booby trapped from the outset with the two-step mechanism that the four Dublin local authorities would firstly have to individually adopt a resolution in favour of holding a plebiscite on the issue.

In the aforementioned The Irish Times article, Harry McGee is overly generous in his conclusion that "Hogan had some great ideas but also a scatter-gun approach to their implementation" (2016a). However a harsher critique is required noting the plan was deliberately sabotaged from the inside by the minister and his officials.

If central government genuinely believes in directly elected mayors, it should fully commit to the idea and legislate for its adoption, rather than taking the kind of hesitant, half-hearted approaches we have seen over the past 15 years.

The Green Party produced an interesting document last year which was quite catchy. It reads:

4 local authorities
4 chief executives
4 mayors
183 councillors
and countless state agencies –
who do you call if you want to call Dublin?

It should be added that in a functioning democracy multiple voices and opinions are to be encouraged. Should one person speak for Dublin?

This is the nub of the issue. There is a need for a debate and greater clarity on the details, especially the powers of the mayor and the relationship between the mayor and the local legislature or council. Ideally, the debate should be evidence-based, as not all of the arguments in favour, or indeed against, directly elected mayors actually stand up to scrutiny. Hambleton, for example, challenges the point that cities need directly elected mayors in order to compete in a rapidly globalising world. He cites Copenhagen, Melbourne and Prague as examples of successful cities which do not have directly elected mayors. This chapter asserts that for a city to compete, it needs effective and strong local government and that may, or may not, include an elected mayor.

There are many different models of directly elected mayors across the world which we should examine. In America, there is a world of difference between the strong and weak mayor versions. In the strong model, the mayor tends to have absolute veto power over the council.

When the author interviewed the directly elected mayor of Albany, he stressed that he worked independently of council. He commented, "I'm not obliged to go to council meetings, thank God". In another fascinating interview with the mayor of Schenectady who was boasting about his powers and the fact that, having inherited what he called a "fiscal train wreck" he was able to turn around the economic fortunes of the city due to his extensive powers. What he failed to mention was that the fiscal train wreck had been created by his predecessor, a mayor with strong powers who had bankrupted the city.

Mayoral models are embedded internationally and have become such a feature of local government that it would be surprising if the introduction of directly elected mayors in Ireland did not return to the political agenda again soon. Certainly, the following are compelling arguments in favour of elected mayors:

- There should be clear political leadership as there is certainty for the public (not to mention the business community and other stakeholders) about who is leading the local area;
- Based on the point above, there should be greater visibility for the mayor and accountability would be enhanced;
- Following a direct election, the mayor would have significant legitimacy.
- There would be increased speed in decision-making;
- The public would possibly take a renewed interest in the affairs of local government;
- Directly elected mayors could emerge as a force for local government reform;
- The mayor would be in a position to address strategic challenges faced by the local area and to drive economic development;
- In larger city regions which might have a metropolitan or 'metro' mayor, there could be several councils working together with a coherent strategic focus to tackle issues such as planning, transportation and infrastructural development.

Individually and collectively these arguments are valid but the point must be made that there is a lack of evidence to support the claims made for elected mayors. As such, it is clearly an area that warrants in-depth study and comparative research. If, and when, directly elected mayors come back onto the political agenda in Ireland, there are lessons which can be learned from other jurisdictions:

- If central government believes in directly elected mayors, it should commit to the idea and legislate for its adoption, rather than taking a hesitant, half-hearted approach;
- There needs to be clarity about the mayoral model that is being introduced;
- The details are important, especially the precise powers of the mayor and the relationship between the mayor and the elected local legislature, i.e. the council.

Directly elected mayors should not be presented as a panacea for local government reinvigoration. It is clear that the Irish local government system needs urgent reform and the introduction of directly elected mayors is only one potential element of that process. To paraphrase Professor Copus, directly elected mayors in Ireland are an idea whose time has not yet come. The various faltering efforts – from the Local Government Act, 2001 to the Local Government Reform Act, 2014 – have been described. While Ireland has yet to embrace the mayoral model, it seems only a matter of time before the idea resurfaces, as strengthening local political leadership is a consistent and dominant international trend. When Ireland next discusses the introduction of directly elected mayors with executive powers, the debate should include a review of the role of the elected council and a fundamental reappraisal of the purpose of local government, based on the devolution of powers to local communities.

There is a need for precision and details in the debate. We can talk about London all we want but that model is based on a directly elected regional mayor and a 25-person assembly. Underneath there are a myriad of local borough councils and the city of London has its own Lord Mayor.

What is meant by a directly elected mayor for Dublin? Is there a justification for keeping the four existing local authorities underneath? Will each of these have its own mayor? Will the city continue to have a separate Lord Mayor? For that matter, what is meant by the Dublin region? Is this the area covered by the existing four local authorities or including neighbouring counties?

At present Dublin's governance is a curate's egg, partly good and partly bad, but is has the potential to be so much better. As C.S. Lewis wrote,

> It may be hard for an egg to turn into a bird:
> it would be a jolly sight harder for it to learn to fly while remaining an egg.
> We are like eggs at present.
> And you cannot go on indefinitely being just an ordinary, decent egg.
> We must be hatched or go bad.

It is high time that Dublin was hatched.

CHAPTER 10
SEX AND THE CITY: GENDER EQUALITY IN THE "NEW POLITICS" OF URBAN AND LOCAL GOVERNANCE

Pauline Cullen

Introduction

This chapter assesses the potential for progressing gender equality through 'new politics' and reformed governance at a local level. The chapter outlines the possibilities that a form of new politics and in particular a directly elected mayor may have for pursuing the increased representation of women in local governance and the substantive representation of women's interests in urban governance. This volume poses questions as to the merits of adopting new forms of local governance inclusive of a directly elected mayor as a way of addressing democratic deficits and supporting forms of economic and social planning.

Various legislative suggestions have been introduced in the Irish context to introduce a system of directly elected mayors. However, analysis suggests that interests at local and national level vary in their support for such proposals (See Callanan in this volume). Debates also continue on the relationship between local government reform and systems of local administration and governance, with particular emphasis on the relative weakness of local government in Ireland (See Quinlivan in this volume). How a directly elected mayor could strengthen the capacity and influence of local government is contingent on the model employed with different systems affording mayors different degrees of power as an executive with a cabinet or with a managerial post and structures (See Quinlivan in this volume). Supporters of directly elected mayors argue for strong mayors with an executive role and high levels of visibility and accountability to constituents that could support devolution from centralised state power (Copus, 2006). Other assessments point to the possibilities that a directly elected mayor can hold in directing forms of strategic collaboration between civil society, private and public interests that can generate innovative responses to public policy problems, including those addressing gender inequality (See O' Donnell in this volume).

Cities and local governance are unique contexts to evaluate gender representation and gender equality. Much analysis of women's influence in governance has taken place on the national level, this chapter examines these processes at the local level in a context with low levels of female representation and complex and contested governance structures. Drawing from research on women in local politics (Childs and Cowey, 2014; Buckley et al., 2015; Farrell and Titcombe, 2016); local administration (Buckley and Hofman, 2015); local government reform and decision making (Ó Broin and Murphy, 2013; Callanan et al., 2014); this chapter will explore local and mayoral governance from a gendered perspective in the Irish context. In theoretical terms local governance will be understood here as a set of gendered organisations, institutions and practices (Acker, 1990)[34]. The context for this work also includes local government reform and alignment processes initiated by the Local Government Reform Act, 2014 for local administration. The chapter begins with an overview of the merits of approaching local and urban governance from a gendered perspective. Next it details scholarship that has examined the implications of directly elected female mayors on policy making. It then outlines the situation with regard to the descriptive or numerical representation of women in governance and recent efforts to assess the experience of women in local governance in Ireland. It then outlines the descriptive representation of women in Dublin City Council. The chapter finishes with a review of efforts to use city political office – in particular the mayoralty - to support gender equality initiatives and detail a series of recommendations that could support a directly elected mayor to pursue gender equality.

It is an interesting time to discuss urban governance and gender. There have been highly publicised elections of a number of first female mayors in cities including Rome and Milan, Barcelona, Prague, Paris and Baghdad. Globally the number of women mayors is rising. However, data on the proportion of women mayors internationally is difficult to assess, a function in part of the variable nature of how the

---

[34] Gendered organisational and Feminist Institutionalist analysis theorises that organisations are not merely gender-neutral sites where gender inequality is reconstituted, but that organisations themselves are gendered, reflecting and reproducing male advantage. All aspects of organisations and institutions, including rules, procedures, and hierarchies, reflect longstanding distinctions between men and women, masculinity and femininity, and power and domination in ways that aid in the reproduction and maintenance of gender inequality (See Acker, 1990 and MacKay, 2014).

office is organised in different contexts. Those directly elected often have the strongest mandates others are the leaders of city councils elected by fellow councillors while others are state appointees. Prominent female mayors have also begun to work together. Barcelona's mayor since June 2015, Ada Colau, elected from the left wing La PAH movement and Anne Hidalgo who became Paris' first female mayor in April 2014 have collaborated on a manifesto that called on European cities to welcome refugees (Rustin 2016b). Sophie Walker the leader of the UK Women's Equality Party contested the 2016 London mayoral race pursuing a strong platform of feminist and gender equality issues (Women's Equality Party 2016). Commentary on the London race has suggested that the presence of a female and feminist identified candidate running alongside two male candidates (Zac Goldsmith Conservative party and Sadiq Khan for Labour) placed pressure on the mainstream parties to pay attention to issues impacting women (Bazeley et al., 2017).

The issue of directly elected mayors has risen to prominence in the UK, particularly, with the introduction of powerful new city region mayors (Copus, 2016; Bazeley et al., 2017). In the United States where 20.4% of mayors are female, a female mayoral caucus exists that has campaigned for the adoption of city ordinances to accept the UN Convention for the Elimination of Discrimination Against Women and the establishment of a city level permanent commission on the status of women (CAWP, 2017). The rise of right wing and populist administrations has also reinvigorated debates around the capacity of city and local governance to reinvigorate a new politics that can engage with issues including climate change, migration and inequality including gender representation (Barber, 2013; Barber, 2017).

Engendering Local and Urban Governance
A gender-sensitive approach to urban governance has two principle objectives; first, to increase women's participation in urban development and, secondly, to foster gender-awareness and competence among both women and men in the political arena and planning practice (Beall, 1996). Engendering local governance reveals that women and men participate in and benefit from local governance in different ways that are shaped by prevailing constructions of gender, whose norms, expectations, and institutional expressions constrain women's access to the social and economic, and thus political resources

of local governance (Beall, 1996). In the context of local and city governance women may have different priorities to men in terms of their use of services. For example, London and many US cities prepare gender audits of transport systems to acknowledge these gendered realities. Transport planning has often disregarded women's priorities because of a focus on mobility rather than accessibility and a preoccupation with the formal sector worker's journey and itinerary. Women's travel needs frequently require transport outside of peak hours and to alternative destinations from those of men (Beall, 1996). Sexual violence and harassment are other reasons women and girls experience cities differently from men. The UN global safe cities initiative includes user surveys and audits of public space aimed at reducing risks of sexual assault. A focus on women can also raise issues pertinent to other under-represented groups, including older people, children, racial and ethnic minorities. Engendering the practice of urban governance also directs attention to broader questions of diversity and civic engagement and affords connections be made between social justice, participatory practice and gender equity (Pini and McDonald, 2011).

Women's Representation in Local and Urban Policy Making

While women populate structures and processes of local governance at a higher proportion than at the national level, they continue to be a minority in senior decision-making roles (Buckley et al., 2015; CEMR, 2016). In the 2014 Irish local elections 21% of those elected to local government were female politicians, significantly below the then EU28 average of 32% for women's representation in local politics (Buckley and Hofman, 2015). Women also predominate in local authority and public service employment. Over 60% of staff in the Irish civil service are female yet they constitute 33% of senior management roles (Department of Public Expenditure and Reform, 2011).

Research has made the link between low levels of female representation in decision making and poor outcomes for women's interests in policy making (Mackay, 2014; Palmeri, 2015). Increasing women's' presence in nominated and elected offices and building capacity and opportunity for women to influence local decision making is seen to deliver solutions to the challenges of social and economic diversity (Cornwall and Goetz, 2005; CEMR, 2016) and to increase transparency and reduce asymmetry at local level (Araujo and Tejedo-Romero, 2016).

There are also arguments that decision making improves when gender parity exists (OECD, 2015; European Commission, 2013). Increasing the representation of women in leadership positions is understood to challenge and shift workplace cultures and provide women with a greater capacity to participate in the development and implementation of legislation, policies and services that affect their lives (Stainback et al., 2016). The promotion of gender equality is suggested to be most impactful when built into budget and (pre) planning stages of policy making at senior levels (Domingo et al., 2015). Increased representation of women in leadership positions including mayoral office, is also suggested to have a symbolic value in role modelling for other women although this is contingent on the presence of women in local authorities and local councils and the experience of women in local governance more generally (Beall, 1996; Smith, 2014). The role of local political experience in securing access to national political office is also relevant in the Irish context where in successive elections the majority of candidates elected were office holders at the local level (Buckley et al., 2015). Research in the American context found that women who served as directly elected mayors were more competitive for higher office (Budd et al., 2016). This work also argued that women who pursue gendered policy agendas were more likely to run for mayor and also more likely to win. Women candidates for a directly elected mayor were in turn helpful in mobilising women voters on the local level and improving female voter turnout (Budd et al., 2016).

Local government with its proximity to women's lives, is uniquely situated to strengthen women's leadership and participation and improve the representation of their interests (Palmeri, 2015). In this sense it is argued women's presence in decision making (descriptive representation by gender) while not guaranteeing that women's interests will be promoted, does increase the likelihood of their substantive representation (the inclusion of women's interests in policy making) (Childs and Krook, 2009: 125-145; Celis et al., 2014).

Female Representation and Participation in Decision Making: Access and Influence

The concept of women's substantive representation is inherently complex (Franceschet, 2015; Celis et al., 2014) and the presence of a critical mass of women in a decision making contexts is understood to only result in changes in policy given certain conditions (Krook and Childs, 2009; Smith, 2015)[35]. These include that women occupy positions of power and that they are enabled to act in politically strategic ways in association with critical actors often in civil society and in structures that support deliberation on and the articulation of women's needs and perspectives (Carbert, 2011; Stokes, 2011) [36]. Whether and how women deliver on women's interests is also contingent on the gendered institutional context where male norms, rules and practices may undermine the ability to integrate women's concerns and perspectives into public policy making. Gendering processes may also silence women by pressuring them to conform to positions taken by men on various political issues or blocking their opportunities to articulate freely their own views (Murray, 2015). Scholars also suggest that without processes that are specifically designed to increase women's involvement in decision-making, women can be excluded from leadership positions in the community, local administration and local government sectors (Farell and Titcombe, 2016; CEMR, 2016).

In their analysis of poor levels of gender parity in local representation and government in Ireland, Buckley and Hofman (2015) refer to 'gendered legacies' and 'institutional norms' created by social and legal obstacles to women accessing work outside the home and

---

[35] Many of the theoretical debates about women's substantive representation have revolved around questions of essentialisation and reification of "women" as a category and whether it is even possible to talk about "women's interests" given the heterogeneity of women as a group (from an intersectional perspective). I argue that we can allow for diversity of women (class, race, ethnicity, spatial location, ablebodiness, sexual orientation etc.) while recognising specific gender interests arising from a common set of responsibilities and roles. Women and men also have overlapping interests.

[36] While individual women may profess personal support for women's interests, the structure and culture of the institutional location, political ideology, social class and other forms of identification and social status also shape when and how women have influence and if they support women's interests

entering into public life in the past [37]. Women do not succeed in gendered bureaucratic organisations for reasons including 'including indirect and direct discrimination, gender stereotyping of senior managerial positions, exclusion from key gendered social networking events and the gender segregation of occupational role' (Lynch and Lyons 2008, 163–4 cited in Buckley and Hofman, 2015). Verge (2010) examines the use of gender quotas in Spain to increase the representation of women in local politics. However, these efforts were restricted to a minority of districts over a certain population and did not extend to more powerful Mayoral or cabinets posts.

Outside of quotas other gender reform strategies to improve gender representation in local government include training, education and promotional campaigns. Carbert (2011) looking at the Canadian case highlighted how women activists and state based feminist organisations used these strategies to increase the representation of rural and minority women in municipal leadership. Despite these efforts gender representation in local governance in Canada remains low with 16% of mayors, and 24% of councillors female, and the odds of having a female mayor decreasing as city size increases. In the United Kingdom Stokes (2011) details how in the 1980s, the establishment of women's committees within local municipalities did provide a dedicated space for women to access leadership roles and have their interests represented. However, these were phased out in the 1990s as part of a broader shift to a more neoliberal governance model marking a reversal in gains for women in these local governance spaces.

Because they are marginalised politically, women's collective strength and their access to positions of influence is then critical to amplify their power (O'Neil and Domino Pinigo, 2016: 11). How women use their political presence is a key issue. Drawing from a quantitative data set of mayoral elections in US cities between 1950-2005, Ferreria and Gyourko (2014) tested for a relationship between the presence of female mayors and women friendly policy outcomes, finding little effect [38]. However they did find 'higher unobserved

---

[37] These authors suggest the application of a gender quota for local political candidates

[38] The same factors that make it more likely or less likely that a female mayor is elected – also correlate with certain types of policies these studies aim to

political skills' for female majors and an increased likelihood of incumbency. In other analysis of large US cities over a ten-year period (1996-2006) Smith (2014) explored the connection between the presence of a female mayor, their power relative to the city council and spending patterns. Utilising a city-level dataset and modelling women's presence as mayors and policy outputs endogenously, she contends that empowered female executives in municipal governments influence expenditure decisions made as part of the federal Community Development Block Grant programme [39]. In her analysis when women obtain leadership positions in municipal government and when the positions they hold have greater power relative to other municipal positions, cities will be more likely to produce policy outputs that are associated with women's interests and needs.

Holding for differences in ideology, social, economic and gender profile of cities and the structural features of governance a clear pattern emerged that women hired other women into key roles and directed spending towards social goals (Smith, 2014). In this assessment, women's presence in governance alone does not guarantee substantive outcomes for women. Rather, it is their level of political incorporation particularly executive incorporation or the extent to which women are positioned to exercise significant influence over the municipal policy making processes. This level of influence works as a key variable that intervenes between the presence of women office holders and the policy responsiveness of women. Smith's overall findings suggest that when women have power and when women are present in different elements of governance, cities become more responsive to women's interests and needs. Crucially, as path dependence is a key element in city spending, if powerful women can change the direction of previous administrations, their impact is felt beyond their immediate term in office (Smith, 2014). Holman's (2013) analysis of the relationship between female mayors, the percentage of female local councillors and spending patterns across a random sample of large US cities also found

---

control for some of these factors such as the % of highly educated people and endogenous factors such as competition between local governments.

[39] In her assessment factors including the length of term served and other variables related to political party affiliation, social class profile of city, % of college educated women; median female income; number of women owned businesses and the political context of the city were included (Smith, 2014).

gendered effects. In this analysis high levels of female representation on city councils and a mayor-council, rather than a mayor–manager, interact with the presence of a female mayor to increase the provision and size of social welfare programmes in cities. She argues that when the proportion of women on the council surpasses 20% this accelerates the influence of the female mayor (Holman, 2013: 711). Ultimately, an empowered female mayor can make a difference for women's interests especially when supported by women office and post holders in local governance.

Gender and Local and Urban Governance in Ireland

While some efforts have been made to audit the gender disparities in local governance in Ireland (Buckley et al., 2015; Farrell and Titcombe, 2016), there is a gap in knowledge and data about the gender composition of local governance and the experience of women working as locally elected officials and in local administration across the country. Women's community development organisations also represent important vehicles for the representation of women's interests at the local level as they work with local governance structures to deliver services and input into policy making (NWCI, 2015). Women councillors also often originate in the community development sector (Buckley et al., 2015). Assessments of proposals for a directly elected mayor point specifically to the potential of such a post to construct meaningful collaborative policy setting spaces where civil society organisations play a significant role (see O'Donnell in this volume). This is particularly relevant in the Irish context where local government in Ireland has developed as a complex networked governance space (Diani, 2015) where civil society and local governance interact in partnership structures that include Public Participation Networks (PPNs), Local Community Development Committee's (LCDCs) and Strategic Policy Committees (SPCs). These structures work as spaces where women in civil society input into local development planning processes. The Local Government Reform Act, 2014 has been criticised for introducing a streamlined and rationalised system of consultation that has worked to increase the complexity rather than the democracy of collaboration for civil society actors with implications for input on women's issues (Harvey et al., 2015; Lloyd, 2015). Analysis suggests

144

specifically, that local government reform alongside austerity has resulted in the loss of a gender perspective in local governance (NWCI, 2015).

Buckley and Hofman (2015) mapped the patterns of gender representation at the local level in Ireland detailing how just one in five councillors are women and how it was 1998 before a woman was appointed to the role of local authority manager, nearly seventy years after men first began to occupy such positions. Just 6 of the 31 councils have a female chair in the 2014/15 council year, with 28 of the 137 local electoral areas represented by all-male slates of councillors. The Local Government Reform Act, 2014 also heralded a 73% reduction in local councils and abolition of town councils which disproportionately affected women. As a function in part of anticipatory responses by political parties to national gender quota legislation enacted in 2016, there were 128 more women candidates contesting the 2014 local elections than in 2009, with the number of women councillors increasing from 146 to 197.

However, wide variations remain in terms of political party selection of women candidates and the geographical representation of women. Following the 2014 local elections, women occupy just under 21% of the 949 council seats in the Republic of Ireland. Notably, 28 of the 137 local electoral areas are represented by all-male slates of councillors, no council reached gender parity and just 6 of the 31 councils had a female chair in the 2014/15 council year (Buckley and Hofman, 2015). Examining women's representation across the thirty-one local authorities in Ireland revealed that only three have achieved a so-called critical mass status of 30% or more women councillors. The implications of these imbalances are significant in the context of how localism shapes candidate selection processes for Dáil elections. In the 2007 and 2011 Dáil elections Buckley et al. (2015) found that 76% of male candidates elected had local government experience while for women the figure was 81%.

The Association of Irish Local Government (AILG) 2016 survey illustrated the significant pressures placed on local councillors and highlighted in part the difficulties facing female county councillors in particular (AILG, 2016). Buckley et al. (2015) found that for rural-based women with care duties additional burdens included the lack of proximity to council and constituent meetings. Dublin City Council (2008) attempted what is the only systematic gendered assessment of women in local government – electorally and as employees. This report found significant deficits in representation and systematic obstacles for women in achieving leadership roles and or influencing policy outputs. These included barriers to women wishing to progress through the organisation; a lack of role models and mentors and low levels of job rotation and or family friendly or work life balance arrangements. In its recommendations it suggested supporting dialogue between community leaders, officials and political office holders to examine interpretations of community development and the effects of Dublin City Council policy on women's lives. It also recommended a commitment to provide on ongoing gender audit of the spread of women and men employed across grades and positions within the City Council. However, men continue to dominate senior management positions in the administrative structures of local authorities (See table 1). In April 2015 six women held the title of local authority chief executive in the Republic of Ireland, accounting for approximately 19% of all chief executives. While 23 local authorities had at least one woman in senior management team and in 13 local authorities women head finance or director of services position, a quarter of all local authorities have no women in the senior management team (Buckley and Hofman, 2015: 91-2).

State initiatives aimed to reform local governance such as In Better Local Government: A Programme for Change (Department of the Environment, Heritage and Local Government, 1996: 6) included a proposal for a special development programme to increase the number of women managers in local authorities. However, this was not implemented (Connelly, 2011: 64 cited in Buckley and Hoffman, 2015). Another initiative Putting People First (Department of the Environment, Community and Local Government (DECLG), 2012) was also weak on concrete proposals to advance women in local government (Buckley and Hoffman, 2015: 95). Guidelines for the composition of other structures, including the SPCs and LCDCs, recommend that they aim for equal and diverse representation but there is no compulsion to achieve gender parity.

Out of 31 LCDCS, 8 have achieved more than 40% female membership, where 4 LCDCs have less than 20% women membership and only 1 LCDC has achieved over 50% female membership (Cullen, 2015; NWCI, 2015; NWCI, 2016). The Fawcett Society, the UK based women's rights organisation alongside the UK's Local Government

Information Unit (LGIU) recent report Local and Equal – does local government work for women? (Bazeley et al., 2017) explored patterns of gender representation across local governance. Mapping the sector, they found that while women make up over 75% of the local government workforce they were 33% of local councillors, 19% of elected mayors and 13% of council leaders. The research also revealed patterns of sexism and gender bias that restricted leadership opportunities for women and inflexible working practices that disadvantaged women with caring responsibilities (Bazeley et al., 2017). The UK does offer an interesting case to assess the relationship between devolution, directly elected mayors and gender representation in local governance. Copus (2016) argues that support for directly elected mayor in the UK is uneven, with national issues and party political identifications combining with continuing imbalances between central and local government that work to limit the appetite for directly elected mayors among the public and constrain directly elected mayors in effecting important change. Bazeley et al. (2017) research on the gendered implications of devolution in the UK and in particular the Northern Powerhouse or Osborne Strategy noted the potential that a commitment to regional directly elected mayors would hold for increasing women's representation. However, they also noted that only 4 of the 16 existing directly elected mayors in England and Wales are women and although 40% of local councillors in the Northern Powerhouse region are women, they made up just 21% of council leaders and directly elected mayors. The strategy was aimed at redistributing power towards the region, yet in only 1 of the 7 chairs of the established and proposed combined authorities in the Northern Powerhouse region are women. Moreover, the Greater Manchester devolution deal was signed by 12 people, all white men, in 2014 (Rustin, 2016a). Of 134 senior leadership roles in the Northern Powerhouse 96 (or 72%) of these are occupied by men (Bazeley et al., 2017). Analysis suggests that historic gender imbalance in senior local government roles, and especially in the roles focused on economic development are a key element in the paucity of female candidates (Rustin, 2017). In the UK local elections in May 2017, six male mayors were elected to lead new combined authorities with no female candidate selected (Local Government Association, 2017). In this context, local government reform has failed to deliver opportunities to improve female representation.

With regard to an assessment of Dublin City Council as a gendered governance context and reflection on the possibilities that a directly elected mayor could hold for improving the descriptive and substantive representation of women. Dublin City Council can claim to have achieved a critical mass of women councillors, ranging from Dún Laoghaire–Rathdown at 43%, South Dublin 33% and Dublin City 32%. Crumlin–Kimmage (67%), Blackrock (67%), Rathfarnham (67%), Castleknock (57%). This reflects a trend in gender representation at the national level, where the highest ratios of women were found in urban areas or large county towns (Buckley and Hofman, 2015). However, as table 1 details senior management within Dublin City Council maintains significant gender deficits.

Table 10.1 Gender Representation of Dublin City Council Senior Management (2016)

	Male	Female
Strategic Policy Committee (Chair)	7	1
Senior Management Team	4	2
Senior Management Group	7	4

This said there are examples of efforts to include gendered perspectives in policy and planning. For example in February 2013, Dublin joined the UN Safe Cities Global Initiative pledging to research and combat sexual harassment and sexual violence against women and girls in public spaces. Dublin City Council conducted user surveys and audits in order to establish gendered patterns of usage and appropriate provisions (Dublin City Council, 2015). Through group interviews and questionnaires, the researchers found that sexual harassment was a persistent problem for women of all ages and backgrounds, identifying specific groups that were targeted more than others including younger women, gay women, homeless women, immigrant women, Traveller women, Roma women, and sex workers. Other initiatives have focused on the economic integration of ethnic minorities and the support for the social inclusion of LGBT people. While DCC has then achieved levels of descriptive representation and advanced some measures to gender its policy making, women office holders lack access to the executive forms of incorporation required to influence policy (Smith, 2014).

Conclusion

Given the deficits in gender representation at local level, how could proposals for a directly elected mayor support greater descriptive and substantive representation of women in local governance? The key arguments advanced for directly elected mayor include increased accountability, an improvement in policy coherence, the attraction of investment and increased legitimacy that would in turn inspire more civic involvement (Copus, 2006). A directly elected mayor would also empower individual councillors to hold a mayor to account (Quinlivan, 2008). A female directly elected mayor may align with this new form of governance as female political leaders are associated with distributed and transformational forms of leadership that support greater transparency and 'new politics' (Tremaine, 2000; Jalalzai, 2015). If empowered and supported by allies, male and female in local governance, a female directly elected mayor could work as a critical actor to advance women's interests (Childs and Krook, 2009).

A brief analysis of the proposals for a directly elected mayor (Quinlivan, 2008) also suggests a variety of opportunities to prioritise gender equality. The introduction of new governance structures, the constitution of an assembly and cabinet could create important opportunities to employ gender quotas to ensure gender parity among local and city councillors and senior management in local administration. Membership of a cabinet could also be contingent on the completion of unconscious gender bias training. There is also scope here regarding independent experts with their role in-putting to a cabinet advising an executive director. Such experts could provide gender expertise on a range of issues including gender budgeting, gender impact assessments of policy making, and gender audits of procurement processes. The proposal to create an assembly that meets in public could also further highlight deficits in gender representation and provide opportunities for civil society organisations working on women's interests to monitor and input in policy setting processes.

A key element of arguments for a directly elected mayor and reformed governance more generally is the opportunity for greater policy coherence and strategic leadership that could in turn help embed processes such as gender mainstreaming. Such actions are not without precedent, London's Mayor Sadiq Kahn appointed women to senior posts in policing and, transport and conducted a gender audit of pay for local administrative posts. In New York Mayor de Balsio instituted a mayor led office to combat domestic violence and a commitment for women to serve in 50% of his administrations leadership positions. Organisations such as the Its Time network, dedicated to improving women's representation in policy making in the US, have produced mayoral guides aimed at promoting gender equality in cities and local government. Recommendations include adopting a city ordinance on UN (CEDAW); establishing a permanent Commission (or Department) on the Status of Women; gender impact assessments to analyse, identify and change existing policies that discriminate against women and girls and commitments to ensure gender equality is embedded in the culture and goals of local administrations and their messaging.

Policy makers and planners, whether women or men, need to be gender-aware in order that women's needs and interests are addressed and women themselves are brought in to the planning process. Reform of local governance including the introduction of a directly elected mayor provide opportunities to create inclusive partnerships in local and urban governance. Any approach to improving democracy and efficiency in local governance need to take account of the obstacles to women's involvement in public life, such as a lack of confidence or skills and the burden of multiple responsibilities. Nor are women the only group to be marginalised from political and planning processes. Diversity is a reality of local and urban development. A gendered approach to representation and planning offers solutions to many of the challenges presented by social and economic diversity.

CHAPTER 11
DO WE REALLY WANT A DIRECTLY ELECTED MAYOR?

Eoin O'Malley

Introduction

In any discussion about mayoral governance in Dublin there is an assumption first, that it is a good thing, that it will solve lots of problems in the city, and second, that the mayor should be directly elected. Particularly as a result of Brexit, there is a realisation that Dublin is not competing with Cork or Limerick, but must compete with other cities such as Amsterdam, Frankfurt and Paris. We can see that many cities and regions maintain lobbying offices in Brussels, for instance, and that cities have become political actors in their own right. There is an increased awareness that cities are the basis and drivers of economic activity, and that the city and its policies can encourage clusters of certain activities. As such cities within the same country can do well or badly as a result, not of national policy, but because of the attributes and policies of the city.

But cities in many countries are constrained by the fact that cities have few policy-making functions. Ireland is at the extreme end of the scale in the level of functions granted to local government by what some see as an overly centralised state (Ó Broin and Jacobson, 2017). Without much autonomy Irish cities have few policy instruments at their disposal to deliver the sorts of changes that the population may want. The few competencies they do have, such as in the area of planning, are quite tightly controlled (Ó Broin and Jacobson, 2010; Moore-Cherry and Tomaney, 2016).

Cities and local government in general control many of the factors that 'make' a place. The answer to the question 'does urban politics matter?' is a certain 'yes' (see for instance Glaeser, 2012). If we think of any 'great' city the feel of the city will be determined by aspects that naturally fit into urban government. At the same time many of the challenges facing states, for instance climate change, security, migration, and globalisation are issues that require local responses. While Ireland's small size means that the Irish government can respond to emerging local problems reasonably quickly, there is a sense that the current model of local administration is inadequate to deal proactively with such challenges.

When we look at cities who are successful at dealing with challenges, for instance, the decline in crime in New York, the redevelopment of city centres or docklands in Baltimore, Manchester or Melbourne, the shift from a dying industrial economy to pharma, finance, arts, design in places such as Milan, or Gothenburg it is difficult to think of successful cases where the role of political leadership wasn't central in co-ordinating or mobilising that shift (Pierre and Peters, 2012: 82).

And so it is felt that a directly elected mayoral system offers cities, particularly Dublin, the opportunity to make itself heard on the world stage. This volume is no exception to that. We often hear the paraphrased quote - 'who do I ring if I want to talk to Dublin?' We want to be able to identify who runs the place. We want someone to be running the city. Directly elected mayors give us that.

The 'direct' in direct election, a bit like in direct democracy, is a 'Yay'- word. It is seen as an unarguable good. Who could not be in favour of giving people a direct say in and, a direct link to, who runs the city? This chapter questions whether direct election is in fact the best approach, and constructs an argument that we might be better off using a political representation model based on a the system we already use in electing Ireland's Taoiseach, namely indirect representative democracy. First the chapter will look at other issues that are important, possibly more important to enable Irish cities to control their fate.

The Basis for Power

Creating a directly elected 'leader' is assumed to deliver leadership. The ceremonial mayoral model extant in Ireland is so devoid of power that no one can seriously think Ireland has democratic local leadership. Local TDs are far more effective leaders and advocates of local affairs, even working across party lines to lobby on behalf of their region, county, or city. Voters, similarly, view their TDs as representatives of the local area. Even in 2011 when the Irish economy was experiencing a crash of unprecedented proportions 38 per cent of voters claimed to base their vote on someone who "would look after the local area" (Marsh and Cunningham, 2011: 185).

We often miscalculate what the sources of social power are. For instance in 1999 the constitution was amended to give constitutional recognition to local government and to ensure that local elections would be held every five years – they had been postponed in the 1980s and 1990s. Stipulating that local elections would be held was obviously and easily justiciable – no government could refuse to hold them again, but giving recognition to local government afforded it no special powers. We know that local government is no more powerful today because of its constitutional status that it had been.

This is because local government's power derives from central government, something known in the US as Dillon's Rule: "Municipal corporations owe their origin to, and derive their powers and rights wholly from the legislature. It breathes into them the breath of life, without which it cannot exist. As it creates, so it destroys" (cited in Kübler and Pagano, 2012: 117). The Irish administrative system, as is noted by many of the authors here, is (possibly pathologically) attached to centralised decision-making. Many authors complain about the desire of the now Department of Housing, Planning and Local Government (in its various historical forms) to micro-manage and its centralising tendencies, in particular in planning, which do not allow bespoke responses to often unique problems.

So, the assumptions that direct election will be empowering and a good thing ignore the more likely important issues of deciding; the relationship between central government and city government, what competencies the mayor might have, what geographical area the mayor might rule over, and the central issue of funding.

The centralising tendencies of government and the dominance of central over local government might be as a result of a classical debate, whereby metropolitan government is characterised by fragmentation and overlapping competencies which are inherently inefficient. An example might be the existence of town councils within the county councils. The response to these problems is to consolidate the institutions, which in Ireland reinforces Dillon's Rule. In other places, such as London we saw the abolition of layers of local government, in that case the Greater London Council.

This fragmentation versus consolidation debate leads many to see inherent problems in Dublin's four council system. How can anyone speak for Dublin when there are four Dublin authorities, four Dublins? This is further complicated given that three of the four Dublins lack any real historical, cultural or popular identity. Independently these councils seem too small to help Dublin to deal with the challenges of being or becoming a global city, but all together become too large to deal with the specific local issues of the village-like nature of certain suburbs.

Had the levels of government been more rationally designed one might see that they could work together via negotiation and co-operation. However, as described in earlier chapters of this volume, current governance arrangements can prompt a tendency towards competition rather than collaboration, and this poses a challenge in agreeing the principle of a mayor for the Dublin region.

There are also cultural attachments to the administrative boundaries: the county boundary. Though the county system was essentially an imperial import, and one that one might have expected the new state to have overthrown with alacrity, perhaps because 'it was there', or path dependency, no decision was taken to remove the county system. Perhaps because the GAA operates on the basis of counties now there is an almost pathological attachment to the county structure.[40]

Voter behaviour within constituencies which cross county boundaries is telling in that voters tend to vote for the candidate within their own county. Changes in constituency boundaries, recommended to ensure proportionality, are opposed most vehemently.

The attachment to county is pathology because the size of counties are so variable that it sometimes makes it difficult for some smaller counties to provide the level of service or maintain expertise in areas that larger counties can. Attempts to consolidate local authorities have failed in Ireland, and in any that have happened they have just been limited to within counties, for instance the merger of Tipperary North and Tipperary South. The attachment to boundaries mean that the normal expansion and governance of some cities, such as Limerick, becomes almost impossible (Callanan, 2017b).

Limerick city is positioned on the border of Clare and close to Tipperary. For the city to control its own expansion, and for it to have its own policies be effective, say to encourage shopping in the city centre, it needs to encompass land beyond its own limited county

---

[40] Callanan (2017b) outlines the resilience of existing county-based structures, highlights the challenges to reform and clearly details that while current boundaries do not provide "the optimum areas for service delivery, effectiveness and convenience, taking into account of modern transport and settlement patterns ... the historical counties themselves attract strong traditional loyalties".

boundary. The 'reform' that took place to merge the services of Limerick City Council and Limerick County Council did not make the logical leap of giving parts of east and south Clare and northeast Tipperary to the city. But even this might not solve the problem, as the long standing debate on fragmentation in local government might suggest that the move to regional government would be more appropriate (Lefèvre and Weir, 2012).

As well as the geography of local government, a significant and unresolved problem is funding. Sub-national government expenditure in Ireland is just ten per cent of overall public expenditure in Ireland (OECD, 2016: 20). Even that money that is directed to and spent by local government might overestimate the power of local government, as for much of it local authorities have limited autonomy. In some areas, such as education, the local authority is merely a paying agent for programmes designed by central government, so the function is delegated rather than seeing power decentralised. The powers of a mayor are dependent upon their given competencies. Currently Irish local government has some competency over planning, but much of the decisions on transport, infrastructure and security are taken nationally. Even those competencies that are devolved to local government are heavily circumscribed. This lack of autonomy and the inability of a metropolitan mayor to raise revenues could render the role ineffectual. In short a directly elected mayor does not derive power from the electorate but from what central government chooses to give it. There is little evidence to suggest that central government would want to cede powers even to a popularly elected leader.

The Forms of Local Leadership
The assumption that having a directly elected mayor will be a good thing that strengthens the city also ignores the fact that we can and do have strong political leaders who are not directly elected. There are broadly three models for city governance. One is the council-manager system we currently have – where the mayor has no executive powers. There's an assumption that it is a bad thing. It certainly isn't very democratic, in the sense that it is not responsive to voters' wishes – there are no clear links between the vote in local elections and local government policy. It is also not very transparent – though that might be due to the absence of real media reporting of city government. It in turn might be a function of the lack of clarity in decision making. The

155

council-manager system of local governance is used in other countries such as Norway and Finland, although it is apparent that Ireland may cede greater responsibilities to the manager than our counterparts.

The second model is the directly elected mayor or mayor-council system which is used in London, European cities such as Rome, and about half of the big US cities including New York and Chicago. Ireland's nearest and most influential neighbours have adopted this system and it's probably for these reasons that we assume this system is the natural fit for us.

However, there can be inconsistencies within this system in the powers of the mayor and therefore the council's control of the legislative and financial functions can vary considerably.

There is a third model. It is a council-elected executive mayor system. The elected councillors appoint a mayor, who has executive functions. As with the directly elected mayor, depending on rules, the mayor's power can vary quite significantly. The system is quite common, used in many northern European cities, such as Amsterdam, Berlin, Stockholm and Paris. The system in France is one with the strongest mayor of all, a position that is sometimes likened to a local monarch (Wollmann and Thurmaier, 2012: 189), and a role which former prime ministers are willing to take.

There is a fourth option, government by committee, where the powers are spread to council committees, and no one figure takes a co-ordinating leadership role. It is criticised for the fragmentation of functions and lacking of clear accountability, and clearly does not solve the leadership problem, so is unlikely to be adopted here.

So which works best? The literature on city government does not have a clear conclusion. So the short answer is, we don't know. But if we approach the question slightly differently, we might have an answer. We can think of the two models, the directly and indirectly elected executive mayors as functional equivalents to the presidential and parliamentary systems at the national level in governments.

And there is a long debate in political science about the relative success of the two systems at delivering democratic stability, human development outcomes, and on a range of other indicators of a country's success. So which should we choose if we are to be guided by the relative performance of presidential or parliamentary systems?

The presidential system, that is the system analogous to directly elected mayor, has some advantages. Candidates are required to present a vision to the public. It puts power in the hands of one person, on the basis of popular election. That means the presidential system is clearer and appears fairer. We all know who we vote for and the person who gets most votes becomes mayor.

Unlike in parliamentary systems, there is no messing about with coalition building that is based on backroom deals that lack transparency and over which the voters have little control - in the so-called smoke-filled rooms. Much of the debate in parliamentary elections is about who will coalesce with whom, a debate that could be avoided in presidential systems. Instead the rival candidates for mayor could debate the issues facing Dubliners and present their competing visions.

The presidential system also weakens the power of parties. Many people dislike parties, and regard them as gatekeepers of political ambition. With a presidential system new leaders can emerge without having to be nominated by a party. It broadens the potential pool for political leadership. This is much less likely in a parliamentary system.

And at a time when people complain that government is unresponsive to their needs, and lack leadership, the mayor could have clear lines of power to deal with certain problems. A suitably empowered mayor might be able to deal with the housing crisis in a way that the local authorities, minister and agencies cannot.

The parliamentary system, that is the indirectly elected mayor, however, has some advantages of its own.

One might seem a weak one, but it might be important. We are used to parliamentarism – it is in our political culture. Political culture governs how we behave and are expected to behave. It changes slowly and doesn't always respond to institutional changes - perhaps not at all, or perhaps not in predictable ways. This is important because picking systems that we are used to means we are less likely to get nasty surprises.

A stronger argument in favour of parliamentarism is the way it divides power. Politics is meant to do at least two things. It should solve collective action problems. That is problems that we are collectively made better off if we are guided to behave in certain ways than if we were left to act individually. The classic example is fishing. Individually we have an incentive to extract as many fish as we possibly can from the seas. We would overfish, making us collectively worse off if fish stocks are depleted. So we are made better off if we are forced to restrict our fishing though policy instruments such as quotas.

Politics is therefore also a mechanism for the resolution of conflicts, such as the fishing one. In parliamentary systems the mechanism for the resolution of conflict is by negotiation, and parties representing different interests compromise, strike deals and build consensus. It must incorporate a wide range of views to reach a decision. This manifests itself in coalitions, with a formal opposition offering alternative policies.

In presidential systems conflict is resolved by the winner, in which the winner takes all. There is less incentive for compromise. You can build systems that restrict the power of the personal executive, and the separation of powers in the US means that US presidents are severely restricted in their capacity for action. Donald Trump may be able to say plenty of obnoxious things, but it is very hard for him to do many of the things he would like to because power is divided.

But that separation of powers that restricts the power of a president or a directly elected mayor can also mean that it is far less decisive than we envisaged. This can take the form of deadlock, as we see in the US, and a certain systemic rigidity, which manifests itself in regime instability, where the only way to relieve the rigidity is a coup, as we frequently saw in Latin America.

So unusually for political science, there is something of a consensus. Most agree that parliamentary systems work better, and in large scale studies of the relative performance of presidential systems to parliamentary systems, the parliamentary systems perform better on a range of measures. This is even the case when we control for the fact that most of Western Europe uses parliamentary systems.

The Decision?
We should be chastened in our assumption that introducing a directly elected mayor will lead to increased leadership in and focus on the needs of our cities. The constitutionalising of local government in 1999 led to no more power because unlike in other countries, such as Sweden, the rights and responsibilities of local government were not also constitutionalised. It is argued that even without specified powers there will be a slow accumulation of power to a political leader on the basis of the legitimacy of the office. The experience of the Irish presidency might guide us here. That role is certainly more visible and

the holders more vocal than they were in the past with the holders having no shortage of ambition and ideological zeal. But the power is limited by the constitution, and is limited to raising issues on the public agenda – applying moral pressure. This would suggest that popular election on its own will not drive the power to the local arena.

We should remember that we can achieve a strong, identifiable executive mayor without direct election. The direct election, though superficially attractive, is something that performs badly in one of the key functions of politics: resolving conflict. Nor does direct election guarantee that effective leadership will flow to the cities that elect them. By contrast the council-elected executive mayoral system is both consistent with the Irish political culture – we are used to it – and it works well in its functionally equivalent form of parliamentary democracy.

REFERENCES

A

Acker, Joan. 1990. 'Gendered institutions: From sex roles to gendered institutions', in *Contemporary Sociology*, Volume 21 (5): 565-569.

Alexander, Alan. 1982. *The Politics of Local Government in the United Kingdom*. London: Longman.

Anderson, Christober J. and Yulia V. Tverdova. 2003. 'Corruption, Political Allegiances, and Attitudes Toward Government in Contemporary Democracies', in *American Journal of Political Science*, Volume 47 (1): 91–109.

Araujo, Joachim and Francisco Tejedo-Romero. 2016. 'Women's political representation and transparency in local governance', in *Local Government Studies*, Volume 42 (6): 885-906.

Association of Irish Local Government (AILG). 2015. *Elected Members Survey Results*. Maynooth: Association of Irish Local Government.

Athlone Boundary Review Committee. 2016. *Report of the Athlone Boundary Review Committee*. Dublin: Department of Housing, Planning and Local Government. Available at: http://www.housing.gov.ie/local-government/reform/boundaries/report-athlone-boundary-review-committee. Accessed 27th July 2017.

B

Bäck, Henry, Hubert Heinelt and Annick Magnier (eds). 2006. *The European Mayor: Political Leaders in the Changing Context of Local Democracy*. Wiesbaden: VS Verlag für Sozialwissenschaften.

Bains, Michael. 1972. *The New Local Authorities: Management and Structure*. London: HMSO.

Barber, Benjamin. 2013. *If Mayors Ruled the World: Dysfunctional Nations and Rising Cities*. New Haven: Yale University Press.

Barber, Benjamin. 2017. *Cool Cities: Urban Sovereignty and the Fix for Global Warming*. New Haven: Yale University Press.

Barringer, Bruce and Jeffrey Harrison. 2000. 'Walking a Tightrope: Creating Value through Interorganisational Relationships', in *Journal of Management* 26 (3): 367-403.

Barrington, Tom. 1991. 'Local Government in Ireland', in *Local Government in Europe: Trends and Developments* (eds) Joyce Johnson and Gerry Stoker. Basingstoke: Macmillan Press.

Bazeley, Andrew, Jennifer Glover, Lauren Lucas, Nan Sloane and Polly Trenow. 2017. *Does Local Government Work for Women? Interim Report of the Local Government Commission*. London: Fawsett Society. Available at: https://www.fawcettsociety.org.uk/wp-content/uploads/2017/04/Does-Local-Government-Work-for-Women-Interim-Report-April-2017.pdf. Accessed at 12th July 2017.

Beall, Jo. 1996. *Urban Governance: Why Gender Matters*. Available at: http://www.gdrc.org/u-gov/doc-whygendermatters.html. Accessed 12th July 2017.

Beesley, Arthur. 2014. 'Divisions over powers of directly elected Dublin Mayor,' in *Irish Times*, 10th February 2014.

Beirne, Maggie. 1993. 'Out of the Bear pit', in *Fortnight*, May 1993.

Bennett, Douglas. 1994. *Encyclopaedia of Dublin*. Dublin: Gill and Macmillan.

Berg, Rikke and Nirmala Rao (eds). 2005. *Transforming Local Political Leadership*. Basingstoke: Palgrave Macmillan.

Bergh, Andreas, Gissur Ó Erlingsson, Mats Sjolin and Richard Ohrvall. 2016. *A Clean House? Studies of Corruption in Sweden*. Lund: Nordic Academic Press

Birnie, Esmond. 2016. 'We can't afford to fall behind in the devolution revolution', in *Belfast Telegraph*, 9th August 2016.

Birrell, Derek and Alan Murie. 1980. *Policy and Government in Northern Ireland: Lessons of Devolution.* Dublin: Gill and Macmillan.

Bjorna, Hilde and Nils Aarsaether. 2009. 'Local Government Strategies and Entrepreneurship', in *International Journal of Innovation and Regional Development,* Volume 2 (1): 50-65.

Blair, Tony. 1998. *Leading the Way: A New Vision for Local Government.* London: Institute of Public Policy Research.

Bochel, Hugh and Catherine Bochel. 2010. 'Local political leadership and the modernisation of local government', in *Local Government Studies,* Volume 36 (6): 723–37.

Boogers, Marcel and Julien van Ostaaijen. 2009. 'Who's the Boss in Oss? Power structures in local governance networks of a small Dutch City'. Unpublished conference paper. EGPA conference, Malta.

Brady, Joseph. 2014. *Dublin 1930-1950: The Emergence of the Modern City.* Dublin: Four Courts Press.

Brennock, Mark. 1999. 'Bill to give new power to directly elected mayors', in *Irish Times,* 30th December 1999.

Bryson, John, Barbara Crosby and Melissa Middleton Stone. 2006. 'The Design and Implementation of Cross-Sector Collaborations: Propositions from the Literature', in *Public Administration Review,* Volume 66 (1): 44-55.

Buckley, Fiona and Caroline Hofman. 2015. 'Women in local government: moving from the margins', in *Administration,* Volume 63 (2): 79-99.

Buckley, Fiona, Mack Mariani, Claire McGing and Timothy White. 2015. 'Is Local Office a Springboard for Women to Dáil Éireann?', in *Journal of Women, Politics & Policy,* Volume 36 (3): 311-335.

Budd, Darlene, Angelique Myers and Thomas Longoria. 2016. 'The role of a gendered policy agenda in closing the mayoral ambition gap: The case of Texas female city council members', in *Journal of Research on Women and Gender*, Volume 6: 81-93.

Burns, James. 1978. *Leadership*. New York: Harper and Row

Byrne, Philip. 2013. 'Directly Elected Mayor for Dublin', in *Local Authority Times,* Volume 17 (3/4): 8.

C

Cahillane, Laura. 2016. *Drafting the Irish Free State Constitution.* Manchester: Manchester University Press.

Callanan, Mark. 2003a. 'Directly Elected Mayors: To Be or Not To Be?' in *Local Authority Times,* Volume 7 (4): 4.

Callanan, Mark. 2003b. 'Where Stands Local Government?', in *Local Government in Ireland – Inside Out* (eds) Mark Callanan and Justin Keogan. Dublin: Institute of Public Administration.

Callanan, Mark. '2008 Green Paper to open up a new front in local government reform?', in *Local Authority Times*, Volume 12 (1&2): 1-9.

Callanan Mark, Ronan Murphy and Aodh Quinlivan. 2014. 'The Risks of Intuition: Size, Costs and Economies of Scale in Local Government', in *The Economic and Social Review*, Volume 45 (3): 371–403.

Callanan, Mark. 2017a. *Local Government in the Republic of Ireland.* Dublin: Institute of Public Administration.

Callanan, Mark. 2017b. 'The Sanctity of the County Jersey in Irish Public Life - Here to Stay or Passed its 'Sell-By' Date?', paper presented at the Political Studies Association of Ireland Annual Conference, Sunday 15th October 2017.

Carbert, Lousie. 2011. 'Making it Happen in Practice: Organized efforts to recruit rural women for local government leadership', in *Women and*

Representation in Local Government: International Case Studies (eds) Barbara Pini and Paula McDonald. London: Routledge.

Carr, Jered. 2015. 'What Have We Learned about the Performance of Council-Manager Government? A Review and Synthesis of the Research', in *Public Administration Review*, Volume 75 (5): 673-689.

Celis, Karen, Sarah Childs, Joanna Kantola and Mona Lena Krook. 2014. 'Constituting Women's Interests through Representative Claims', in *Politics and Gender*, Volume 10: 149-174. .

Center for American Women in Politics (CAWP). 2017. *Women Mayors in U.S. Cities 2017*. Available at:

http://www.cawp.rutgers.edu/levels_of_office/women-mayors-us-cities-2017. Accessed June 12th 2017.

Cheshire, Paul, Max Nathan and Henry Overman. 2014. *Urban Economics and Urban Policy – Challenging Conventional Policy Wisdom*. Cheltenham: Edward Elgar.

Childs, Sarah and Philip Cowley. 2011. 'The Politics of Local Presence: Is there a Case for Descriptive Representation?', in *Political Studies*, Volume 59 (1): 1–19.

Childs, Sarah and Mona Lena Krook. 2009. 'Analyzing Women's Substantive Representation: From Critical Mass to Critical Actors', in *Government and Opposition*, Volume 44 (2): 125-145.

Clark, Mary and Raymond Refaussé. 1993. *Directory of Historic Dublin Guilds*. Dublin: Dublin Public Libraries.

Clark, Mary. 2013. 'Daniel O'Connell and Dublin's quest for a new mayoral image, 1841-71', in *Leaders of the City – Dublin's first citizens 1500-1950* (eds) Ruth McManus and Lisa-Marie Griffiths. Dublin: Four Courts Press.

Clark, Mary. 2015. *The Mansion House, Dublin: 300 Years of History and Hospitality*. Dublin: Dublin City Council.

Coaffee, Jon and Peter Lee. 2016. *Urban Resilience – Planning for Risk, Crisis and Uncertainty*. London: Palgrave.

Coakley, John. 2011. 'Political Culture', in *Politics in the Republic of Ireland* (eds) John Coakley and Michael Gallagher. London: Routledge.

Commission For Local Democracy. 1995. *Taking Charge: The Rebirth Of Local Democracy*. London Municipal Journal Books

Connolly, Michael and Colin Knox. 1988. 'Recent political difficulties of local government in Northern Ireland', in *Policy and Politics*, Volume 16 (2): 89 – 97.

Copus, Colin. 2004a. *Party Politics and Local Government*. Manchester: Manchester University Press.

Copus, Colin. 2004b. 'Directly-elected mayors: a tonic for local governance or old wine in new bottles?', in *Local Government Studies*, 30 (4): 576–588.

Copus, Colin. 2006. *Leading the localities: Executive Mayors in English local governance*. Manchester: Manchester University Press.

Copus, Colin. 2010. 'English Local Government: Neither Local Nor Government', in *Territorial Consolidation Reforms in Europe*, (eds) Pavel Swianiewicz. Budapest: Open Society Institute.

Copus, Colin. 2011. 'Elected Mayors in English Local Government: Mayoral Leadership and Creating a new Political Dynamic', in *Lex Localis*, Volume 9 (4): 335-351.

Copus, Colin. 2013. 'Elected mayors: An idea whose time has not yet come does not make it a bad idea', in *Policy & Politics*, Volume 41 (1): 128-131.

Copus, Colin, Angel Iglesias, Miro Hacek, Michal Illner and Anders Lidstrom. 2016. 'Have Mayors Will Travel: Trends and Developments in the Direct Election of the Mayor: A Five-Nation Study', in *Local Public Sector Reforms in Times of Crisis: National Trajectories and*

International Comparisons (eds) Sabine Khulmann and Geert Bouckaert. London: Palgrave Macmillan.

Copus, Colin. 2016. Presentation to NorDubCo conference, *New Politics and Policy in the City – Mayoral Governance of the Dublin City*. Dublin City University.

Collins, Neil. 1987. *Local Government Managers at Work*. Dublin: Institute of Public Administration.

Collins, Neil and Aodh Quinlivan. 2005. 'Multi-level governance', in *Politics in the Republic of Ireland* (eds) John Coakley and Michael Gallagher. London: Routledge.

Commission of the European Union. 2013. *Women in Economic Decision-Making in the EU: Progress report, A Europe 20:20 Initiative*. Brussels: European Union. Available at: http://ec.europa.eu/justice/gender-equality/files/women-on-boards_en.pdf. Accessed 12th July 2017.

Corcoran, Donal. 2009. 'Public policy in an emerging state: The Irish Free State 1922-25', in *Irish Journal of Public Policy*, Volume 1 (1): 11-17.

Cornwall, Andrea and Anne Marie Goetz. 2005. 'Democratising Democracy: Feminist Perspectives', in *Democratization*, Volume 12 (5): 783-800.

Council of Europe. 2011. *Local Government in Critical Times: Policies for Crisis, Recovery and a Sustainable Future*. Strasbourg: Centre of Expertise for Local Government Reform.

Council of Europe. 2013. *Local Democracy in Ireland*. Strasbourg: Centre of Expertise for Local Government Reform. Available at: https://rm.coe.int/168071a75c. Accessed 25th July 2017.

Council of European Municipalities and Regions (CEMR). 2015. *European Charter for Equality of Women and Men in Local Life*. Brussels: CEMR.

Crosby, Barbara and John Bryson. 2005. *Leadership for the Common Good: Tackling Public Problems in a Shared-Power World*. San Francisco: Jossey-Bass.

Cudden, Jamie. 2015. 'City Regions and the changing role of local government in supporting their economic growth potential', in *Administration*, Volume 63 (2): 149-176.

Cullen, Pauline. 2015. *Making Women Central to Local Government: Report on Focus Group Consultation*. Dublin: NWCI.

D

Daly, Mary. 2006. *The Slow Failure: Population Decline and Independent Ireland, 1920–1973*. Madison: University of Wisconsin Press.

Davies, Anna. 2007. 'A wasted opportunity? Civil society and waste management in Ireland', in *Environmental Politics*, Volume 16 (1): 52-72.

Denters, Bas, and Lawrence E. Rose (eds). 2005. *Comparing Local Governance: Trends and Developments*. Basingstoke: Palgrave Macmillan.

Department for Communities (NI). 2016. *District Council Rate Statistics 2016/17*, Circular LG 13/16. Belfast: Department for Communities.

Department for Communities and Local Government (UK). 2011. *Second phase of the Local Government Resource Review: Terms of Reference*. London: HMSO. Available at: http://webarchive.nationalarchives.gov.uk/20120919134742/http://www.communities.gov.uk/documents/localgovernment/pdf/1933423.pdf. Accessed 13th July 2017.

Department of the Environment, Heritage and Local Government. 2008. *Stronger local democracy: Options for Change*. Dublin: Department of the Environment, Heritage and Local Government.

Department of the Environment, Community and Local Government. 2012. *Putting People First*. Dublin: Department of the Environment, Community and Local Government.

Department of the Environment, Transport and the Regions (DETR). 1998a. *Modernising Local Government: Local Democracy and Community Leadership*. London: Department of the Environment, Transport and the Regions.

Department of the Environment, Transport and the Regions (DETR). 1998b. *Modern Local Government: In Touch with the People.* London: Department of the Environment, Transport and the Regions.

Department of the Environment, Transport and the Regions (DETR). 1999. *Local Leadership: Local Choice.* London: Department of the Environment, Transport and the Regions.

Department of Local Government, Transport and the Regions (DLTR). 2001. *Strong Local Leadership: Quality Public Services.* London: Department of Local Government, Transport and the Regions.

Department of the Environment (DoE). 1991. *Local Government Review: The Structure of Local Government in England: A Consultation Paper*. London: Department of the Environment.

Department of Justice and Equality. 2013. *Towards Gender Parity in Decision-Making in Ireland: An Initiative of the National Women's Strategy 2007-2016*. Dublin: Department of Justice and Equality.

Department of Public Expenditure and Reform. 2011. *Survey on Gender in Public Employment*. Dublin: Department of Public Expenditure and Reform.

Diani, Mario. 2015. *The Cement of Civil Society: Studying Networks in Localities*. Cambridge: Cambridge University Press.

Dickson, David. 2014. *Dublin: The Making of A Capital City*. London: Profile Books.

Dollery, Brian E., Joseph Garcea and Edward C. LeSage (eds). 2008. *Local Government Reform: A Comparative Analysis of Advanced Anglo-American Countries*. Cheltenham: Edward Elgar.

Domingo, Pilar, Rebecca Holmes, Tam O'Neil, Nicola Jones, Kate Bird, Anna Larson, Elizabeth Presler-Marshall and Craig Valters. 2015. *Women's Voice and Leadership in Decision-Making: Assessing the Evidence*. London: Overseas Development Institute. Available at: https://www.odi.org/publications/9514-womens-voice-leadership-assessment-review-evidence. Accessed 12th July 2017.

Dublin Chamber of Commerce. 2015. *Submission: Directly Elected Mayor for Dublin*. Available at: http://www.dubchamber.ie/docs/policy-reports/submission-on-directly-elected-mayor.pdf. Accessed 25th July 2017.

Dublin Chamber of Commerce. 2017. *President Calls for Debate on Unification of 4 Dublin Councils*. Available at: http://www.dubchamber.ie/news/press-releases/news/display-news/2017/02/03/president-calls-for-debate-on-unification-of-4-dublin-councils. Accessed 25th July 2017.

Dublin City Council. 2008. *Every Step of the Way: Women Accessing Power in Dublin City*. Dublin: Dublin City Council.

Dublin City Council. 2015. *Report of the Scoping Study for Dublin City Council Safe City Programme*. Dublin: Dublin City Council.

Dublin City Council. 2017. *Lord Mayors and Deputy Lord Mayors of Dublin*. Available at: https://data.dublinked.ie/dataset/lord-mayors-and-deputy-lord-mayors. Accessed 22nd September 2017.

Dublin Journal. 1763. 23rd July 1763.

Dublin Journal. 1782. 5th September 1782.

Dublin Journal. 1791a. 6th September 1791.

Dublin Journal. 1791b. 22nd October 1791.

Dublin Journal/Saunder's Newsletter, 17th July 1793.

E

Elcock, Howard. 2001. *Political Leadership*. Cheltenham: Edward Elgar.

Elcock, Howard and John Fenwick. 2007. 'Comparing Elected Mayors', in *International Journal of Public Sector Management*, Volume 20 (3): 226-238.

Emerson, Newton. 2016. 'Belfast needs an ambitious vision, not more party political strategies,' in *Sunday Times*, 20th November: 25.

F

Farrell, Catherine and Sarah Titcombe. 2016. 'Gender and the experiences of local electoral members – A focus on Wales', in *Local Government Studies*, Volume 42 (6): 867-884.

Fenwick, John and Howard Elcock. 2014a. *Has the introduction of directly elected mayors advanced or detracted from democratic innovation in English local government?* Available at: http://www.democraticaudit.com/2014/03/06/has-the-introduction-of-directly-elected-mayors-advanced-or-detracted-from-democratic-innovation-in-english-local-government/. Accessed 25th July 2017.

Fenwick, John and Howard Elcock. 2014b. 'Elected Mayors: Leading Locally', in *Local Government Studies*, Volume 40 (4): 581-599.

Franceschet, Susan. 2015. 'Gendered Institutions and Women's Substantive Representation: Female Legislators in Argentina and Chile', in *Gender, Politics and Institutions: Towards a Feminist Institutionalism* (eds) Mona Lena Krook and Fiona Mackay. Houndmills: Palgrave Macmillan.

Freedman Consulting LLC. 2013. *The Collaborative City - How partnerships between public and private sectors can achieve common goals.* Available at: https://www.bbhub.io/dotorg/sites/2/2015/07/The_Collaborative_City.pdf. Accessed 17th July 2017.

G

Garrard, John (eds). 2007. *Heads of the Local State: Mayors, Provosts and Burgomasters since 1800.* Aldershot: Ashgate.

Givan, Paul. 2016. *Minister's Statement: Progress of the Regeneration Bill - 22 November.* Belfast: Department for Communities.

Glaeser, Edward. 2012. *Triumph of the City: How Our Greatest Invention Makes Us Richer, Smarter, Greener, Healthier, and Happier.* New York: Penguin.

Gordon, Ian and Nick Buck. 2005. 'Cities in the New Conventional Wisdom,' in *Changing Cities – Rethinking Urban Competitiveness, Cohesion and Governance* (eds) Nick Buck, Ian Gordon, Alan Harding and Ivan Turok. Basingstoke: Palgrave Macmillan.

Government of Ireland. 2008. *Green Paper on Local Government: Stronger Local Democracy – Options for Change.* Dublin: Stationery Office.

Government of Ireland. 2012. *Putting People First: Action Programme for Effective Local Government.* Dublin: Stationery Office.

Greasley, Stephen and Gerry Stoker. 2008. 'Mayors and Urban Governance: Developing a Facilitative Leadership Style', in *Public Administration Review,* Volume 68 (4): 722–730.

Griffiths, Lisa-Marie and Ruth McManus. 2013. 'An Introduction to Dublin's First Citizens', in *Leaders of the City – Dublin's first citizens 1500-1950* (eds) Ruth McManus and Lisa-Marie Griffiths. Dublin: Four Courts Press.

Gross, Jill Simone and Robin Hambleton. 2007. 'Global Trends, Diversity and Local Democracy', in *Governing Cities in a Global Era – Urban Innovation, Competition and Democratic Reform* (eds) Robin Hambleton and Jill Simone Gross. Basingstoke: Palgrave.

H

Hambleton, Robin. 2003. 'The New City Management', in *Globalism and Local Democracy – Challenge and Change in Europe and North America* (eds) Robin Hambleton, Hank Savitch and Murray Stewart. Basingstoke: Palgrave Macmillan.

Hambleton, Robin. 2013. 'Elected mayors: An international rising tide?', in *Policy & Politics*, Volume 41 (1): 125-128.

Hambleton, Robin. 2014. *Leading the Inclusive City: Place-Based Innovation for a Bounded Planet*. Bristol: Policy Press.

Hambleton, Robin and David Sweeting. 2014. 'Innovation in Urban Political Leadership: Reflections on the Introduction of a Directly Elected Mayor in Bristol, UK', in *Public Money and Management*, Volume 34 (5): 315-322.

Harvey, Brian. 2015. 'Local and Community Development in Ireland - An Overview', in *The Changing Landscape of Local and Community Development in Ireland: Policy and Practice Conference Proceedings*. Cork: Institute for Social Sciences in the 21st Century (ISS21). Available at: https://www.ucc.ie/en/media/research/iss21/TheChangingLandscapeof LocalandCommunityDevelopmentinIrelandPolicyandPractice.pdf. Accessed 12th July 2017.

Haslam, Richard. 2003. 'Origins of Irish Local Government', in *Local Government in Ireland Inside Out* (eds) Mark Callanan and Justin Keogan. Dublin: Institute of Public Administration.

Hayes, Maurice. 1967. 'Some Aspects of Local Government in Northern Ireland', in *Public Administration in Northern Ireland* (eds) Edward Rhodes. Aldershot: Edward Elgar.

Hayes, Brian. 2016. 'A Mayor to make Dublin a fair city', in *Sunday Times*, 6th November 2016.

Henry, Brian. 1994. *Dublin Hanged: Crime, Law Enforcement and Punishment in Late Eighteenth-Century Dublin*. Dublin; Irish Academic Press.

Hewison, Grant. 2008. *Effective Relationships and Collaborative Arrangements between Central and Local Government - A Report prepared for the Waitakere City Council.* Available at: http://www.waitakere.govt.nz/havsay/pdf/royalcommission/effective-relationships.pdf. Accessed 17th July 2017.

Hill, Jacqueline. 1997. *From Patriots to Unionists: Dublin Civic Politics and Irish Protestant Patriotism, 1660-1840.* Oxford; Clarendon Press.

Hill, Jacqueline. 2001. 'The shaping of Dublin government in the long eighteenth century', in *Two capitals: London and Dublin, 1500-1840 (Proceedings of the British Academy)* (eds) Peter Clark and Raymond Gillespie. Oxford: Oxbow Books.

Himmelman, Arthur. 1996. 'On the Theory and Practice of Transformational Collaboration: From Social Service to Social Justice', in Chris Huxham (ed.) *Creating Collaborative Advantage.* London: SAGE.

HMSO. 1967. *Committee on the Management of Local Government Vol. I, Report of the Committee.* London: HMSO.

HMSO. 1986. *Committee of Inquiry into the Conduct of Local Authority Business, Report of the Committee into the Conduct of Local Authority Business.* London: HMSO.

HMSO. 1993. *Community Leadership and representation: Unlocking the Potential, The Report of the Working Party on the Internal Management of Local Authorities in England.* London: HMSO.

HM Treasury and Department of Communities and Local Government (UK). 2010. *Total Place: a whole area approach to public services.* London: Office of Public Sector Information. Available at: http://webarchive.nationalarchives.gov.uk/20130125093102/http://www .hm-treasury.gov.uk/d/total_place_report.pdf. Accessed 17th July 2017.

Holinshed, Raphael. [1577] 1965. *Holinshed's Chronicles England, Scotland, and Ireland.* New York: AMS.

Holman, Mirya. 2013. 'Sex and the City: Female Leaders and Spending on Social Welfare Programs in U.S. Municipalities', in *Journal of Urban Affairs*, Volume 36 (4): 701-715.

Howard, Joanna, and David Sweeting. 2007. 'Addressing the Legitimacy of the Council-Manager Executive in Local Government', in *Local Government Studies*, Volume 33 (5): 633-656.

Hudson, Bob, Brian Hardy, Melanie Henwood and Gerard Wistow. 1999. 'In Pursuit of Inter-Agency Collaboration in the Public Sector: What is the Contribution of Theory and Research?', in *Public Management*, Volume 1 (2): 235-60.

Huxham, Chris and Siv Vangen. 2005. *Managing to Collaborate: The Theory and Practice of Collaborative Advantage*. New York: Routledge.

Hyland, Paul. 2012. 'Directly elected mayor still a possibility for Dublin – but not before 2014', in *The Journal*, 17th October 2012. Available at: http://www.thejournal.ie/directly-elected-mayor-dublin-638915-Oct2012/. Accessed 24th July 2017.

I

International City/County Management Association. 2014. *The Municipal Year Book 2014*. Washington DC: ICMA.

Irish Times. 2017. 'Elected mayors must have power' (editorial), in *Irish Times*, 15th December 2017.

J

Jalalzai Farida 2016. 'Shattered Not Cracked: The Effect of Women's Executive Leadership', in *Journal of Women, Politics & Policy*, Volume 37 (4): 439-463.

Jepp, Andrew. 2011. 'A problem shared', in *Public Finance*. Available at: http://www.publicfinance.co.uk/2011/02/a-problem-shared-by-andrew-jepp. Accessed 17th July 2017.

Jesús García, María and Alessandro Sancino. 2016. 'Directly Elected Mayors vs Council Appointed Mayors – Which Effects on Local

Government Systems? A Comparison between Italy and Spain', in *Theoretical Foundations and Discussions on the Reformation Process in Local Governments* (eds) Ugur Sadioglu and Kadir Dede. Hershey: IGI Global.

John, Peter. 2001. *Local Governance in Western Europe*. London: Sage.

K

Kavanagh, Adrian 2014. 'What results tell us about Greens, gender and reform', in *Irish Independent*, 26th May 2014.

Keane, John. 2009. *The Life and Death of Democracy*. London: Simon and Schuster.

Keles, Rusen. 2016. 'The Normative Base of Local Government: Progress in Local Democracy and the Reformation Process', in *Theoretical Foundations and Discussions on the Reformation Process in Local Governments* (eds) Ugur Sadioglu and Kadir Dede. Hershey: IGI Global.

Kelly, Olivia. 2013. 'Dublin Mayor should take over transport and waste – report,' in *Irish Times*, 16th December 2013.

Kelly, Olivia. 2014. 'Fingal councillors play ball and block plebiscite,' in *Irish Times*, 31st March 2014.

Keogan, Justin. 2003. 'Reform in Irish Local Government', in *Local Government in Ireland – Inside Out* (eds) Mark Callanan and Justin Keogan. Dublin: Institute of Public Administration.

Kenny, Liam. 2003. 'Local Government and Politics', in *Local Government in Ireland – Inside Out* (eds) Mark Callanan and Justin Keogan. Dublin: Institute of Public Administration.

Kenny, Liam. 2004. *From Ballot Box to Council Chamber: A Guide to Ireland's County, City and Town Councillors 2004-2009*. Dublin: Institute of Public Administration.

Keogh, Dermot. 2013. 'There is a Crisis in the Irish State'. Paper delivered at the Magill Summer School 2013. Available at:

http://www.macgillsummerschool.com/there-is-a-crisis-in-the-irish-state/. Accessed 25th July 2017.

Kissane, Bill. 2001. 'Democratic Consolidation and Government Changeover in the Irish Free State', in *Commonwealth & Comparative Politics*, Volume 39 (1): 1- 22.

Klausen, Kurt Klaudi and Annick Magnier. 1998. 'The New Mandarins of Western Local Government – Contours of a New Professional Identity?', in *The Anonymous Leader: Appointed CEOs in Western Local Government* (eds) Kurt Klaudi Klausen and Annick Magnier. Odense: Odense University Press.

Knox, Colin and Paul Carmichael. 2006. 'Bureau Shuffling? The Review of Public Administration in Northern Ireland', in *Public Administration*, Volume 84 (4): 941-965.

Knox, Colin and Paul Carmichael. 2010. 'Devolution in Northern Ireland', in *Public Money and Management*, Volume 30 (2): 82-83.

Knox, Colin. 1998. 'Local government in Northern Ireland: emerging from the bear pit of sectarianism?', in *Local Government Studies*, Volume 24 (3): 1–13.

Knox, Colin. 2007. 'Symbolism or Substance? The Mayoralty in Northern Ireland', in *Heads of Local State: Mayors, Provosts and Burgomasters since 1800* (eds) John Garrard. Aldershot: Ashgate Publishers.

Knox. Colin. 2010. 'Local Government', in *Devolution and the Governance of Northern Ireland* (eds) Colin Knox. Manchester: Manchester University Press.

Kotter, John P. and Paul R. Lawrence. 1974. *Mayors in Action: 5 Approaches to Urban Governance*. New York: John Wiley and Sons.

Kübler, Daniel and Michael A. Pagano. 2012. 'Urban Politics as Multilevel Analysis', in *The Oxford Handbook of Urban Politics* (eds)

Karen Mossberger, Susan E. Clarke and Peter John. Oxford: Oxford University Press.

Kuhlmann, Sabine and Hellmut Wollmann. 2014. *Introduction to Comparative Public Administration: Administrative Systems and Reforms in Europe*. Cheltenham: Edward Elgar.

Kukovic, Simona, Colin Copus, Miro Hacek, and Alasdair Blair. 2015. 'Direct Mayoral Elections in Slovenia and England: Traditions and Trends compared', in *Lex Localis*, Volume 13 (3): 697-718.

L

Labour Party. 1995. *Renewing Democracy, Rebuilding Communities*. London: Labour Party.

Lacey, Dermot. 2017. *Cathaoirleach's Paper on Regional Governance – A New Regional Approach to One Dublin*. Dublin: Irish Labour Party.

Lapuente, Victor. 2010. 'A tale of two cities: bureaucratisation in mayor-council and council-manager municipalities', in *Local Government Studies,* Volume 36 (6): 739–57.

Leach, Stephen and David Wilson. 2000. *Local Political Leadership*. Bristol: Policy Press.

Leach, Stephen. 2006. *The Changing Role of Local Politics in Britain*. Bristol: Policy Press

Leach, Stephen 2010. *Managing in a Political World: The Life Cycle of Local Authority Chief Executives*. Basingstoke: Palgrave MacMillan

Lefèvre, Christian and Margaret Weir. 2012. 'Building Metropolitan Institutions', in *The Oxford Handbook of Urban Politics* (eds) Karen Mossberger, Susan E. Clarke and Peter John. Oxford: Oxford University Press.

Lennon, Colm. 1989. *The Lords of Dublin in the Age of Reformation*. Dublin: Irish Academic Press.

Lindblom, Charles. 1959. 'The science of 'muddling through', *Public Administration Review*, Volume 19 (2): 79-88.

Litton, Helen. 2013. 'Kathleen Clarke, first woman lord mayor of Dublin', in *Leaders of the City – Dublin's first citizens 1500-1950* (eds) Ruth McManus and Lisa-Marie Griffiths. Dublin: Four Courts Press.

Lloyd, Aiden. 2016. *How Government's Putting People First policy will effectively put socially excluded people last.* Available at: http://www.sdcp.ie/download/pdf/local_government_reform_paper.pdf?issuusl=ignore. Accessed 12th July 2017.

Local Government Association. 2017. *Directly Elected Mayors.* Available at: http://www.local.gov.uk/topics/devolution/directly-elected-mayors. Accessed 12th July 2017.

Loughlin, John, Frank Hendriks and Anders Lidström. 2011. 'Introduction – Subnational Democracy in Europe: Changing Backgrounds and Theoretical Models', in *The Oxford Handbook of Local and Regional Democracy in Europe* (eds) John Loughlin, Frank Hendriks and Anders Lidström. Oxford: Oxford University Press.

M

Mackay, Fiona. 2014. 'Remembering the Old, Forgetting the New: 'Nested Newness' and the Limits of Gendered Institutional Change', in *Politics & Gender*, Volume 10 (4): 459-471.

Macrory Report. 1970. *Review Body on Local Government in Northern Ireland* –Cmd 546. Belfast: Her Majesty's Stationery Office.

Magre, Jaume and Xavier Bertrana. 2007. 'Exploring the Limits of Institutional Change: The Direct Election of Mayors in Western Europe', in *Local Government Studies*, Volume 33 (2): 181-194.

Maguire, Martin. 1998. *Servants to the Public: A History of the Local Government and Public Services Union 1901-1990*. Dublin: Institute of Public Administration.

Manning, John. 2016. 'Local support for an elected Mayor', in *The Irish Independent*, 3rd December 2016.

Mayor's Taskforce on Toronto Community Housing. 2015a. *Improved Living at Toronto Community Housing: Priority Action*. Available at: http://homelesshub.ca/resource/improved-living-toronto-community-housing-priority-actions. Accessed 26th July 2017.

Mayor's Taskforce on Toronto Community Housing. 2015b. *Getting it Done: Real Change at Toronto Community Housing*. Available at: https://www.torontohousing.ca/about/policies-programs/Documents/Board%20Scorecard.160729.final%20including%20sustainment.pdf. Accessed 27th July 2017.

MacCarthaigh, Muiris and Mark Callanan. 2007. 'The Mayoralty in the Republic of Ireland', in *Heads of the Local State: Mayors, Provosts and Burgomasters since 1800* (ed) John Garrard. Aldershot: Ashgate.

MacCarthaigh, Muiris. 2009. 'The Relevance of Irish Local Government', in *Studies*, Volume 98 (389): 43-57.

MacCarthaigh, Muiris. 2012. 'Governance and accountability: the limits of new institutional remedies' in *Irish Governance in Crisis* (ed) Niamh Hardiman. Manchester: Manchester University Press.

McAdam, Noel. 2001. 'Vote early and vote twice – the general election will not be the only show in town on polling day', in *Belfast Telegraph*, 18th May 2001.

McGee, Harry. 2016a. 'Why Dublin needs mayor with real powers', in *Irish Times*, August 12th 2016.

McGee, Harry. 2016b. 'Plans set to be revived for directly elected mayors', in *Irish Times*, June 13th 2016.

McGee, Harry. 2017a. 'Government to support directly elected Dublin mayor', in *Irish Times*, November 14th 2017.

McGee, Harry. 2017b. 'Cork and Dublin to have directly elected mayors', in *Irish Times*, December 9th 2017.

McGuire, Michael. 2006. 'Collaborative Public Management: Assessing What We Know and How We Know It', in *Public Administration Review*, Volume 66 (1): 33-43.

Miller, David. 2002. *The Regional Governing of Metropolitan America*. Boulder: Westview Press.

Moore-Cherry, Niamh and John Tomaney. 2016. 'Fair City? Planning Challenges in Post-Crisis Dublin', in *Town and Country Planning*, Volume 85 (6): 239-243.

Mouritzen, Poul-Erik and James A. Svara. 2002. *Leadership at the Apex: Politicians and Administrators in Western Local Governments*. Pittsburgh: University of Pittsburgh Press.

N

National League of Cities (NLC). 2006. *Guide to Successful Local Government Collaboration in America's Regions*. Available at: https://datatoolkits.lincolninst.edu/subcenters/regional-collaboration/pubs/RC_for_Local_Govts_2006.pdf. Accessed 17th July 2017.

National Women's Council of Ireland (NWCI). 2015. *Making Women Central to Local Government*. Dublin: NWCI.

National Women's Council of Ireland (NWCI). 2016. *What Women Want: Consultation Checklist for Local Community Development Committees*. Dublin: NWCI.

Needham, Richard. 2017. 'If Belfast is to be a world class city of the 21st century…you need leadership for that to happen', in *Belfast Telegraph*, 9th January 2017.

New South Wales Department of Local Government. 2007. *Collaboration and Partnerships between Councils*. Sydney: NSW Department of Local Government. Available at:

http://www.olg.nsw.gov.au/sites/default/files/Collaboration-and-Partnerships-between-Councils-A-Guidance-Paper.pdf. Accessed 17th July 2017.

Norris-Tirrell, Dorothy and Joy Clay. 2010. *Strategic collaboration in public and non-profit administration*. New York: CRC Press.

O

Ó Broin, Deiric. 2005. *Participatory Democracy, Representation and Accountability: Some Lessons from Ireland's Community Sector*. PhD Dissertation. University College Dublin.

Ó Broin, Deiric and Eugene Waters. 2007. *Governing Below the Centre: Local Governance in Ireland*. Dublin: TASC/New Island.

Ó Broin, Deiric and David Jacobson (eds). 2010. *Local Dublin Global Dublin: Public Policy in an Evolving City Region*. Dublin: Glasnevin Press

Ó Broin, Deiric and Mary P. Murphy (eds). 2013. *Politics, Participation and Power - Civil Society and Public Policy in Ireland*. Dublin: Glasnevin Press.

Ó Broin, Deiric and Peadar Kirby (eds). 2015. *Adapting to Climate Change – Governance Challenges*. Dublin: Glasnevin Press.

Ó Broin, Deiric and David Jacobson (eds). 2017. *Local Governance, Development and Innovation – Rebuilding Sustainable Local Economies in Ireland*. Dublin: Glasnevin Press.

O'Donoghue, Paul. 2017. 'Dublin's main business group says one elected mayor should lead the whole region, in *Business Fora* 3rd February 2017. Available at: https://fora.ie/dublin-directly-elected-mayor-2-3220680-Feb2017/. Accessed 25th July 2017.

O'Dowd, Liam, Bill Rolston and Mike Tomlinson. 1980. *Northern Ireland: Between Civil Rights and Civil War*. London: CSE Books.

Office of the Deputy Prime Minister. 2004. *The Future of Local Government: Developing a Ten Year Vision*. London: OPDM.

Office of the Deputy Prime Minister. 2005. *Vibrant Local Leadership*. London: OPDM.

O'Halloran, Marie and Michael O'Regan. 2016. 'Bill to introduce directly elected Dublin mayor progresses', in *Irish Times*, 22nd November 2016.

O'Loughlin, Brendan. 2016. 'Councillors Meet To Discuss A Directly Elected Mayor For Dublin', in *Evening Herald*, 24th October 2016.

O'Malley, Eoin. 2011. *Contemporary Ireland*. Basingstoke: Palgrave Macmillan.

O'Neil, Tam and Domingo, Pilar. 2016. *Women and Power: Overcoming barriers to leadership and Influence*. London: Overseas Development Institute. Available at: https://www.odi.org/sites/odi.org.uk/files/resource-documents/10443.pdf. Accessed 12th July 2017.

Oonan, Chris. 2017. 'Dublin's problems will not be solved by an elected mayor', in *Irish Times*, 29th December 2017.

Organisation for Economic Co-operation and Development (OECD). 2014 *Women, Government and Policy Making in OECD Countries: Fostering Diversity for Inclusive Growth*. Paris: OECD Publishing.

Organisation for Economic Co-operation and Development (OECD). 2016. *Subnational governments around the world: structure and finance - A first contribution to the Global Observatory on Local Finances*. Paris: OECD

Orr, Kevin. 2004. 'If Mayors are the Answer then What was the Question?', in *Local Government Studies*, Volume 30 (3): 331-344.

Osborne, George and Michael Bloomberg. 2017. 'Strong Mayors can help UK take on the world: with increased powers, towns and cities will find local answers to the effects of globalization', in *The Times*, 27th February 2017.

Ostrower, Francie. 2005. 'The Reality Underneath the Buzz of Partnerships: The Potentials and Pitfalls of Partnering', in *Stanford Social Innovation Review*, Volume 3 (1). Available at: https://ssir.org/articles/entry/the_reality_underneath_the_buzz_of_part nerships. Accessed 17th July 2017.

P

Page, Stephen. 2004. 'Measuring Accountability for Results in Interagency Collaborative', in *Public Administration Review*, Volume 64 (5): 591-606.

Pakenham, Thomas and Valerie Pakenham. 1988. Dublin: A Traveller's Companion. London: Constable and Company.

Palmeri, Sonia. 2015. *Measuring Women's Participation in Local Government*. UN Women: United Nations Publications Agency. Available   at: https://unstats.un.org/unsd/gender/Mexico_Nov2014/Session%206%20 UNW%20ppt.pdf. Accessed 12th July 2017.

Peters, Thomas and Robert Waterman, R. 1982. *In search of excellence: Lessons from America's best-run companies*. New York: Harper.

Pierre, Jon and Guy B. Peters, 2012. 'Urban Governance', in *The Oxford Handbook of Urban Politics* (eds) Karen Mossberger, Susan E. Clarke and Peter John. Oxford: Oxford University Press.

Pike, Andy. 2017. 'Metro-mayors: claims and evidence', paper presented at the CURDS and RGS-IBG panel, 'Metro Mayors: next steps for devolution in England', Thursday 30th March 2017. Available at: https://blogs.ncl.ac.uk/curds/. Accessed 12th July 2017.

Pini, Barbara and Paula McDonald (eds). 2011. *Women and Representation in Local Government: International Case Studies*. London: Routledge.

Pleschberger, Werner. 2016. 'Democratic Preferences of the Indirectly Elected Mayor, Open or Locked-In: A Contribution to the 'Difference Hypothesis', in *Theoretical Foundations and Discussions on the Reformation*

Process in Local Governments (eds) Ugur Sadioglu and Kadir Dede. Hershey: IGI Global.

Q

Quinliven, Aodh. 2000. 'Local Government Bill 2000 – Implications for Municipal Authorities. Another False Pregnancy?' in *Administration*, Volume 48 (3): 10-20.

Quinlivan, Aodh. 2008. 'Reconsidering Directly Elected Mayors in Ireland: Experiences from the United Kingdom and America', in *Local Government Studies*, Volume 34 (5): 609-623.

Quinlivan, Aodh. 2015a. 'The 2014 Local Elections in the Republic of Ireland', in *Irish Political Studies*, Volume 30 (1): 132-142.

Quinlivan, Aodh. 2015b. 'The development of the Irish management system and the move towards directly elected mayors', in *Administration*, Volume 63 (2): 101–117.

Quinlivan, Aodh. 2017. 'Reforming local government: Must it always be democracy versus efficiency?', in *Administration*, Volume 65 (2): 109-126.

Quinn, Brid. 2015. 'Local government reform – Plus ça change, plus c'est la meme chose?', in *Administration*, Volume 63 (2): 7-29.

R

Rao, Nirmala. 2005. *Councillors and the New Council Constitutions*. London: ODPM.

Redmond, Janet. 2013. 'Sir Daniel Bellingham, Dublin's first lord mayor, 1665', in *Leaders of the City – Dublin's first citizens 1500-1950* (eds) Ruth McManus and Lisa-Marie Griffiths. Dublin: Four Courts Press.

Reid, Lorna. 2004. 'City must have an elected mayor', in *Irish Independent*, 6th February 2004.

Royal Commission on Local Government in Greater London. 1960. *Report of the Royal Commission on Local Government in Greater London (1957-1960)*. London: HMSO.

Rhodes, Rod. 1996. 'The new governance: governing without government', in *Political Studies*, Volume 44 (4): 652-667.

Rhodes, Rod and Paul t'Hart. 2014. *The Oxford Handbook of Political Leadership*. Oxford: Oxford University Press.

Roberts, Nancy. 2001. 'Coping with Wicked Problems: The Case of Afghanistan', in *Learning from International Public Management Reform Volume 11, Part 2* (eds) Lawrence Jones, James Guthrie and Peter Steane. New York: JAI Press.

Roche, Desmond. 1982. *Local Government in Ireland*. Dublin: Institute of Public
Administration.

Rodriguez-Rose, Andrés. 2009. 'Are city regions the answer', in *The Future of Regional Policy* (ed) John Tomaney. London: The Smith Institute.

Rousseau, Jean-Jacques. 1762. *The Social Contract*. London: Wordsworth.

RTÉ. 2017. 'Waterford and south Kilkenny boundary change proposal sparks row', RTÉ 9th February 2017. Available at: https://www.rte.ie/news/2017/0209/851338-boundary-waterford-kilkenny/. Accessed 27th July 2017.

Rustin, Susanna. 2016a. 'Where are the women? The 'pale, male' council leaders driving the northern powerhouse', in *The Guardian* 3rd February 2016.

Rustin, Susanna. 2016b. 'Can cities be feminist? Inside the global rise of female mayors', in *The Guardian* 12th October 2016.

S

Sadioglu, Ugur and Kadir Dede. 2016. *Theoretical Foundations and Discussions on the Reformation Process in Local Governments*. Hershey: IGI Global.

Sandford, Mark. 2016. *Directly-elected Mayors* (House of Commons Briefing Paper No. 05000). Westminster: House of Commons Library.

Schaap, Linze, Harry Daemen, and Arthur Ringeling. 2009. 'Mayors in Seven European Countries: Part II. Performance and Analysis', in *Local Government Studies*, Volume 35 (2): 235-251.

Seanad Éireann. 2003. *Local Government Bill 2003: Second stage*, 26th February,
Seanad Debates, 171 (12).

Sheehy, Eamon. 2003. 'City and County Management', in *Local Government in Ireland: Inside Out* (eds) Mark Callanan and Justin Keogan. Dublin: Institute of Public Administration.

Simpson, John. 2015. 'Why Council Chief needs bold plans for Belfast's future', in *Belfast Telegraph*, 18th August 2015.

Smith, Adrienne. 2014. 'Cities Where Women Rule: Female Political Incorporation and the Allocation of Community Development Block Grant Funding', in *Politics and Gender*, Volume 10 (3): 313-340.

Sorensen, Eva and Jacob Torfing. 2005. 'Network Governance and Post-Liberal Democracy', in *Administrative Theory and Praxis*, Volume 27 (2): 197–237.

Stainback, Kevin, Sibyl Kleiner and Sheryl Skaggs. 2016. 'Women in Power: Undoing or Redoing the Gendered Organization?', in *Gender and Society*, Volume 30 (1): 109-135.

Stapleton, Patricia. 2013. 'James Carroll: a Pragmatic Protestant mayor in the early seventeenth century', in *Leaders of the City – Dublin's first citizens 1500-1950* (eds) Ruth McManus and Lisa-Marie Griffiths. Dublin: Four Courts Press.

Stoker, Gerry, Francesca Gains, Peter John, Nirmala Rao and Alan Harding. 2003. *Implementing the 2000 Act with Respect to New Council Constitutions and the Ethical Framework: First Report.* London: ODPM.

Stokes, Wendy. 2011. 'Missing from the Picture: Women's Initiatives in English Local Government', in *Women and Representation in Local Government: International Case Studies* (eds) Barbara Pine and Paul McDonald. London: Routledge.

Stone, Clarence. 1995. 'Political Leadership in Urban Politics', in *Theories of Urban Politics* (eds) David Judge, Gerry Stoker and Hal Wolman. London: SAGE.

Svara, James. 1987. 'Mayoral Leadership in Council-Manager Cities: Preconditions versus Preconceptions', in *The Journal of Politics*, Volume 49 (1): 207–27.

Svara, James, and Christopher Hoene. 2008. 'Local Government Reforms in the United States', in *Local Government Reform: A Comparative Analysis of Advanced Anglo-American Countries* (eds) Brian E. Dollery, Joseph Garcea, and Edward C. LeSage, Jr. Cheltenham: Edward Elgar.

Sweeting, David and Robin Hambleton. 2016. Mayoral governance in Bristol: An initial assessment of impacts, Policy Papers, Bristol University. Available at: http://www.bristol.ac.uk/media-library/sites/policybristol/documents/mayoralgovernance.pdf. Accessed 28th August 2017.

Sweeting, David. 2017. *Directly Elected Mayors in Urban Governance: Impact and Practice.* Bristol: Policy Press.

T

Torfing, Jacob, Eva Sorensen and Trine Fotel. 2009. 'Democratic Anchorage of Infrastructural Governance Networks: the Case of the Femern Belt forum', in *Planning Theory*, Volume 8 (3): 282–308.

Travers, Tony. 2011. *Directly Elected Mayors: Guaranteeing Better Urban Governance?,* paper presented at the Dublin Policy Institute. Available at: https://www.tcd.ie/policy-institute/assets/pdf/DF_Travers_Dec11.pdf. Accessed 24th July 2017.

Tremaine, Marianne. 2000. 'Women mayors say what it takes to lead: setting theory against lived experience', in *Women in Management Review*, Volume 15 (5/6): 246-252.

V

Verge, Tània 2010. 'Gendering Representation in Spain: Opportunities and Limits of Gender Quotas', in *Journal of Women Politics and Policy*, Volume 31 (2): 166-190.

Vision Zero. 2016. *Collaborating across departments to achieve Vision Zero*. Available at http://visionzeronetwork.org/wp-content/uploads/2016/05/Cross-dept-collaboration.pdf. Accessed 24th July 2017.

Vision Zero. 2017. Two-Year Action Strategy: San Francisco's roadmap to safer streets. Available at: http://visionzerosf.org/about/two-year-action-strategy/. Accessed 24th July 2017.

W

Wainwright, Martin. 2002. 'Donnygate scandal ends in jail terms', in *The Guardian*, 13th March 2002.

Walker, Brian. 2012. *A Political History of the Two Irelands – From Partition to Peace*. Basingstoke: Palgrave.

Wallace, Ciarán. 2013. 'A rather mild sort of rebel: J.P. Nannetti', in *Leaders of the City – Dublin's first citizens 1500-1950* (eds) Ruth McManus and Lisa-Marie Griffiths. Dublin: Four Courts Press.

Walsh, Jim. 2014. 'Reflections on Fifty Years of National and Regional Planning in Ireland', in *The Journal of Spatial Planning in Ireland*, Volume 4: 69-75.

Webb, Andrew. 2015. 'Why cities should drive growth and not rely on Stormont', in *Belfast Telegraph*, 24th November 2015.

Wollman, Hellmut. 2008. 'Reforming local leadership and local democracy: the cases of England, Sweden, Germany and France in comparative perspective', in *Local Government Studies*, Volume 34 (2): 279-298.

Wollmann, Helmut and Kurt Thurmaier. 2012. 'Reforming Local Government Institutions and New Public Management', in *The Oxford Handbook of Urban Politics* (eds) Karen Mossberger, Susan E. Clarke and Peter John. Oxford: Oxford University Press.

Women's Equality Party. 2016. *Sophie Walker: The Power of Four Million.* Available at: http://www.womensequality.org.uk/sophie_for_london. Accessed 12th July 2017.

Z

Zimmerman, Joseph. 1994. 'One County Becomes Three Counties', in *Administration*, Volume 42 (4): 374-395.

Zimmerman, Joseph. 2006. 'Executive-Council Relations in England and Ireland', in *Current Municipal Problems*, Volume 33 (2): 196-225.

Zurich Municipal and IPSOS Mori. 2010. *Tough Choices: Different perspectives on long term risks facing the public sector and wider civil society.* Available   at: http://www.zurich.co.uk/newworldofrisk/toughchoice/toughchoice.ht m. Accessed 24th July 2017.

Zurich Municipal. 2011. *A new world of risk: rising areas of challenge in a changing local government landscape.* Available at: http://www.zurich.co.uk/internet/newworldofrisk/sitecollectiondocum ents/ newworldofrisk/newworldofriskexecutivesummary.pdf. Accessed 24th July 2017.

Also Available from Glasnevin Publishing

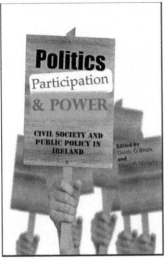

Politics, Participation & Power
Edited by Deiric O'Broin and Mary
Murphy
ISBN-13: 978-1-908689-19-1

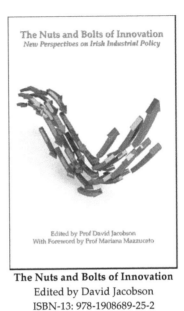

The Nuts and Bolts of Innovation
Edited by David Jacobson
ISBN-13: 978-1908689-25-2

**Awaken the Genius Within: A Guide to
Lifelong Learning Skills**
Samuel A Malone
ISBN-13: 978-1-908689-24-5

Degrees of Nonsense
Edited by Brendan Walsh
ISBN-13: 978-1-9086891-02-3

Also Available from Glasnevin Publishing

Adapting to Climate Change
Edited by Deiric O'Broin and Peadar Kirby
ISBN-13: 978-1908689-30-6

Innovation in the Social Economy
Edited by Deiric O'Broin and Mary Hyland
ISBN-13: 978-1908689-27-6

Irish Theatre and its Soundscapes
Edited by H. Mikami & N. Yagi
ISBN-13: 978-1-908689-28-3

The Beginner's Guide to Android Game Development
by James Cho
ISBN-13: 978-1-9086891-26-9

Lightning Source UK Ltd.
Milton Keynes UK
UKHW012330290519
343533UK00001B/24/P

9 781908 689351